YOUR KNOWLEDGE HAS VALUE

Sebastian Kleinschmager

A Controlled Experiment for Measuring the Impact of Aspect-Oriented Programming on Software Development Time

GRIN Publishing

Bibliographic information published by the German National Library:

The German National Library lists this publication in the National Bibliography; detailed bibliographic data are available on the Internet at http://dnb.dnb.de .

Imprint:

Copyright © 2009 GRIN Verlag, Open Publishing GmbH
Print and binding: Books on Demand GmbH, Norderstedt Germany
ISBN: 978-3-656-31863-7

This book at GRIN:

http://www.grin.com/en/e-book/199337/a-controlled-experiment-for-measuring-the-impact-of-aspect-oriented-programming

GRIN - Your knowledge has value

Since its foundation in 1998, GRIN has specialized in publishing academic texts by students, college teachers and other academics as e-book and printed book. The website www.grin.com is an ideal platform for presenting term papers, final papers, scientific essays, dissertations and specialist books.

Visit us on the internet:

http://www.grin.com/

http://www.facebook.com/grincom

http://www.twitter.com/grin_com

A Controlled Experiment for Measuring the Impact of Aspect-Oriented Programming on Software Development Time

Bachelor Thesis at the Institute of Computer Science and Business

Information Systems, University of Duisburg-Essen

Chair of Data Management Systems and Knowledge Representation

Sebastian Kleinschmager

Angewandte Informatik – Systems Engineering

Date of submission: 22.01.2009

Eidesstattliche Erklärung

Hiermit versichere ich, dass ich die vorliegende Arbeit ohne Hilfe Dritter und nur mit den angegebenen Quellen und Hilfsmitteln angefertigt habe. Ich habe alle Stellen, die ich aus den Quellen wörtlich oder inhaltlich entnommen habe, als solche kenntlich gemacht. Diese Arbeit hat in gleicher oder ähnlicher Form noch keiner Prüfungsbehörde vorgelegen.

Essen, am 22.01.2009

Abstract

In this document, a controlled experiment on aspect-oriented programming that was performed in the context of this bachelor thesis is described and evaluated. The experiment was designed to make the overall performance of developers using object-orientation and aspect-orientation on a number of tasks comparable. The primary focus of the experiment laid on whether aspect-orientation has a positive impact on the development time when comparing its performance with the performance of the object-oriented approach on the same task.

Zusammenfassung

Dieses Dokument beschreibt und wertet ein kontrolliertes Experiment aus, welches im Rahmen der Bachelorarbeit durchgeführt wurde. Das Experiment wurde aufgesetzt, um die allgemeine Arbeitsleistung von Entwicklern bei der Nutzung des objektorientierten und des aspektorientierten Ansatzes für eine Anzahl an Aufgaben vergleichbar zu machen. Dabei wurde der primäre Fokus darauf gelegt messbar zu machen, ob die Aspektorientierung einen positiven Einfluss auf die Entwicklungszeit im Vergleich zur Objektorientierung bei der gleichen Aufgabe hat.

Directory of Figures

Directory of Tables

Directory of Listings

Table of Contents

1. Introduction

"Time is money" is what many people state when considering the aspect of time in modern businesses. Many cost prediction models and actual prices for various products (especially in the area where human service and creativity are playing a major role) are based on time as a central factor. This applies to a large part of the software industry, where the time which developers need to finish the software is a critical factor in almost any software project. The technique of aspect-oriented programming could present a possibility to save a large amount of time, especially for redundant code in larger projects.

This work introduces a controlled experiment that analyzes the development costs in terms of additional development time, caused by the specification of redundant code in the object-oriented programming language Java in comparison to the aspect-oriented programming language AspectJ, which is essentially an add-on for the Java language. Chapter two describes the motivation and the background of the study, trying to argue on the importance of empirical research in this area. Chapter three summarizes some historical background about empiricism, the methods associated with today's empirical research (like controlled experiments), and a short introduction to aspect-oriented programming and the AspectJ implementation of that technique. Chapter four explains the experiment's setup, the specific tasks and their different solutions in aspect-oriented and object-oriented programming. Chapter five explains and presents most of the experiment results from the raw data to the aggregated forms and the statistical and explorative approaches that were done with the data. After a discussion of the experiments results and validity thoughts in chapter six, chapter seven summarizes some related work in the field of studies on aspect-orientation. Finally, chapter eight concludes this work.

2. Motivation and Problem Description

Aspect-oriented programming has been introduced as a major step forward in software development. Some even proposed that

 "AOP could be the next step in the steady evolution of the OO paradigm, or perhaps it will evolve into a completely new paradigm independent of OO"[1],

making it possible to solve difficult problems affecting larger parts of software in less time than it would take using exclusively procedural or object-oriented programming. From looking at its conception, it seems especially well-suited to avoid writing redundant and repeating lines of code which appear on different occasions in the program's code. The study described in this work was therefore focused on redundant code and repetitive tasks, where the progress can be measured easily in time.

All of this sounds like it is a great achievement for the field of software engineering, but as so often in the young computer science, it has still not been tried to strengthen these claims using empirical studies and controlled experiments. Regrettably, this does not only apply to aspect-orientation as a relatively new technique, but to nearly all software engineering methods and techniques. In software engineering, empirical research makes up only a very small amount of all research work and publications. This might be seen as a dangerous development when simultaneously looking at the great impact the field of computer science and business information systems has on everyday life. Basili[2] and Tichy[3] both argue in that direction. Today, vehicles, weapons, machines, air planes, space craft and nearly every other electrical or mechanical system is somehow controlled, observed or at least influenced by software. Modern technology has grown exponentially and towards being nearly completely software relied in such a short time span (about 30 years), that it might be considered extremely careless not to try to validate the use of software engineering methods, techniques, languages and products using empirical research. Not to mention the potential cost and loss of time that could be avoided by differentiating good from bad methods (even if results can only be based on the situation and context). For software development is still a process dominated by human creativity and brains and therefore costs for personnel make up the bulk of the development budgets (attempts on using industrial methods for producing software still have to prove their worth). A lot of time and money is wasted on projects that are never finished or finished way after deadline, on

---

[1] (Highley, et al., 1999), p. 2
[2] (Basili, et al., 2007) and (Basili, 2007), for example. Basili and his colleagues have written many publications on the role and use of empirical studies and experimentation in software engineering
[3] (Tichy, 1997)

faulty software and the correction of these faults, on software that is not accepted by the client or user, not to mention potential risks and costs through security leaks and their exploitation. Unfortunately, there have been nearly no studies on the cost of writing redundant code either.

So to make an own bold claim: There is a huge lack of empirical research in software engineering to back up many assumptions that are made about methods and techniques. One reason might be that empirical research always consumes time and resources, most of the time more than literature study and collecting arguments does. Even for the object-oriented paradigm[1], which has been around for quite some time now, there have been only a handful of studies and experiments trying to strengthen the object-oriented claim of being better suited as an approach to programming[2]. The rationale behind this is often the statement that it fits the way the human brain works. Most people would agree that this argument makes sense and it definitely does. Still, some more studies backing that statement up need to be done.

Hence, this experiment was motivated by all the above grievances and the need for more empirical research. The main motivation was to try to back up or falsify the assumption that aspect-orientation decreases the time needed to write redundant code, but in a rather explorative matter, not trying to concentrate on rejecting or hardening one single hypothesis. One of the central questions was: When would aspect-orientation be the technique providing an advantage in time, and when would the plain object-oriented approach be the better choice and would it even be possible to tell at all? To go a little further, it was tried to find a break-even point depending on task complexity and redundancy, which could be taken as an estimated predictor for anyone trying to assess which technique to use in a given situation, which is why a very fine-grained and basic approach was taken. Another part of the motivation was that as a side-effect of the overall data collection procedure, a large set of data for the process and time consumption of writing redundant code in object-oriented Java was gathered and could be analyzed and used in further studies.

There are also other facets of development that aspect-orientation has an impact on. For example, aspects provide clean design separation and modularization of the so-called crosscutting concerns, which are parts of the software that cannot be cleanly encapsulated into one single class or component (because they crosscut multiple components and code needs to be inserted at these spots to have the crosscutting work as wanted). Modularization of crosscutting concerns can

---

[1] Most people use the word paradigm as a replacement for technique, approach or concept, even if it differs from the word's original meaning. As its original meaning was to represent an underlying concept or a principle agreed by everyone on the matter, it can still be used in software engineering, but people should be aware of its usage in a wrong sense.

[2] The paper of Josupeit-Walter (Josupeit-Walter, 2008) summarizes most of the studies on object-orientation. None of them really managed to back everything that is said about its benefits.

enhance readability, maintainability and flexibility of applications. But aspects also add an increasing amount of complexity to a program. Especially if aspects get tangled into each other, more than one aspect weaves itself into the same place of code and on top of that the dynamic features of aspects are used, which can be very confusing to write and understand. This can make debugging applications crosscut by many aspects a burden or even nearly impossible. Some of the studies mentioned in the related work chapter are concerned with these facets of aspect-orientation and (Highley, et al., 1999) provides a critical analysis of the aspect-oriented approach in general. Thus, this work will only focus on the code redundancy removal and time saving.

3. Experiment Background

3.1. A short summary on Empiricism and Experimentation

3.1.1. What is meant by Empiricism?

The term empiricism is derived from a Greek word meaning "based on experience" and is used in two different contexts: The philosophical and the scientific.

In philosophy, a theory of knowledge[1] says that any real knowledge that can be gained has to be gathered by experiencing and perceiving things with the human senses. This ultimately implies that human beings cannot gain knowledge and ideas out of themselves just by "thinking", which is the concept of another field of philosophy. These two schools of thinking are called empiricism (knowledge arises from experience) and rationalism (knowledge can be gained by reasoning). As a matter of fact, many would agree that they do not exist in the real world in their most radical interpretation, and as a discussion of them is far out of the scope of this thesis, they will not be covered deeper. Interested readers might want to take a look into philosophical literature on both matters.

The more common term of empiricism is used in the modern sciences, its meaning being derived and closely related to the philosophical term. It is used to characterize the methodology of research which tries to strengthen or falsify (it can never prove) scientific theories and hypotheses using experiments or observations of reality, which ultimately leads back to the philosophical notion of learning by experience and observation. Empirical research is especially widespread in the natural and social sciences, as well as in medicine and the pharmaceutical area of research.

3.1.2. Research and Experimentation methods

This chapter's information is primarily based on the work of Prechelt[2] (and the summary of Josupeit-Walter[3]), who concentrated his evaluation and description of empirical research methods on these methods fit to be used in software engineering. The social sciences use other and more detailed categorizations for these methods and are in many matters more precise in their description and implementation.[4] Nevertheless, for this work, the focus will stay on the methods presented by

---

[1] The whole field of theory of knowledge concerns itself with knowledge, its nature, how it is gained, etc. See http://en.wikipedia.org/wiki/Epistemology
[2] (Prechelt, 2001)
[3] (Josupeit-Walter, 2008)
[4] Interesting books to read for anyone interested in detailed information on empirical research methods: (Bortz, et al., 2002), which is very thorough and precise, (Rogge, 1995), which gives a good summary and short explanation or (Christensen, 1977), which is more focused on the experimental approach.

Prechelt. Most of these research methods are based on observation, either through qualitative manual approaches or automated quantitative ones.

3.1.2.1. Case Studies or Benchmarks

Case studies are commonly used to evaluate tools or methods using a controlled but typical environment for their implementation. They mostly consist of one or more tasks or use cases the participants have to fulfill using certain methods or tools, sometimes to evaluate a single method or tool or sometimes to compare two different approaches. The results can be qualitative or quantitative, depending on the implementation of the study. Case studies, in contrast to controlled experiments (explained in more detail later), do not try to keep all possible variable factors constant, which means that all the factors influencing the outcome of the study can possibly have a great impact on the results and make them very indeterministic or complicate the reconstruction of their development because of the many interdependencies. All the same, case studies are still useful for a rough and efficient evaluation of certain approaches or technologies.

To summarize, their advantages lie in their ease of implementation and general application possibilities, while their drawbacks lie in their sometimes unreliable results possibly not giving insights or conclusions.

A special case of case studies are benchmarks, which are standardized case studies which only result in quantitative data. Benchmarks are commonly used to create results that can be compared directly to other implementations of the same benchmark (as it is done in many hardware tests, where a benchmark program is run on computers with different hardware to make their overall performance or the performance of a single device comparable) or to create template data that represents a threshold which certain devices, tools or methods have to fulfill for quality testing.

3.1.2.2. Field Studies

Unlike case studies, benchmarks or controlled experiments, field studies are implemented in the field, meaning real software projects in the industry and are designed as an accompanying observation of specific factors, processes, behaviors or situations in these projects. Field studies try not to influence the observed projects and processes as to not distort the results. They have the advantage that they can be used to observe even complex situations, which would be too time-consuming or complicated to implement in a controlled environment, or if the scientists want to observe unaltered real life situations. But these advantages lead to a drawback comparable to that of case studies, but in a much stronger way: Their results are really hard to transform into a general hypothesis and the whole field study description can get very complex because of the complex circumstances.

3.1.2.3. Controlled Experiments

Of all research methods, controlled experiments try to exert the most control on the experiment's implementation and circumstances. In the optimal case, only one or a few factors are left open as variables, everything else is kept as a constant. These experiments are the hardest to design and implement, as they require thorough planning and disciplined implementation. The setup is generally well defined and only these factors which are the focus of the experiments observations are kept variable. Controlled experiments therefore have a high validity and can easily be reproduced many times (when following the exact setup and implementation), producing reliable and comparable results. Their biggest disadvantage is their large cost in time and work for preparation, buildup and evaluation.

3.1.2.4. Polls

Polls (sometimes called interviews) are easy to implement and to evaluate, and can therefore be used to evaluate facts over a large number of people. However, they suffer from results that are hard to interpret and can be very unreliable, as every submitted answer is a completely subjective rating or evaluation of the specific person. And as many persons tend to have large number of different opinions and views, polls tend to have a large variability in the range of answers, especially when open[1] questions are used. Poll results tend to be more reliably the more persons are included and if the range of questioned persons is representative for certain groups (like an even ratio of software developers and project managers).

3.1.2.5. Meta-Studies

Meta studies take a number of other studies on a certain topic and try to evaluate whether there are differences or similarities between these studies' results and whether there are certain gaps in all data and if unanswered questions remain. They tend to produce less work than most other studies, as anyone carrying out a meta-study mainly has to do investigative work on the results and essays of the original experiments' executors. Their most important aspect is the resulting summary of a possible large field of other works, which can be used by other scientists to get an overview of the current level of research on the topic.

---

[1] Open questions leave the answer to the reader, closed questions give a list of concrete answers or a range of ordinal ratings the reader has to choose from (some allow to pick only one answer, some allow more than one).

3.1.3. Empirical research in Software Engineering – Specifics and Dangers

As stated above, software development is still a process dominated by human creativity and brains. Its mechanisms therefore do still elude a complete understanding and are very hard to measure and capture through observation and data collection. As Prechelt has written in his book, there are many specifics of empirical research and controlled experiments to be considered in software engineering. He states that for many controlled experiments, the most important variable to control is the variation among all participants' approaches and performance on a problem (which is an especially big variation for programming or modeling tasks). The wide range of experience with modeling, programming, programming languages and development tools between software developers, which is the very nature of software development and still eludes any quantitative way of measuring it, makes the results of empirical experiments generally hard to predict or interpret. Empirical research in software engineering is still at its beginning and researchers are still far from being able to handle and control these variations in a way that would make them able to produce very reliable results in most situations. These are some of the reasons why computer scientists tend to stay away from empirical research (Tichy summarizes 16 excuses used most to avoid experimentation in software engineering in his paper that was already cited above: (Tichy, 1997)).

Even the object-oriented approach, which is currently the most used in industry and academics, has not been validated thoroughly[1]. Some even argue that there are still problems in the idea of object-orientation.[2]

3.2. Aspect-Oriented Programming

3.2.1. Aspect-Orientation in General

Object-oriented Programming has had an amazing triumphal procession in the past years, both in the academic world as well as in the industrial development practice. It still has its drawbacks and is sometimes not sufficient for solving a specific set of problems. In 1997, Kiczales and his colleagues published the paper (Kiczales, et al., 1997) which introduced aspect-oriented programming as a modified approach on solving specific problems in software development. The idea was that certain functional parts of software crosscut an application or at least large parts of it (like logging, which is the most worn example for aspect-orientation, tracing, security, synchronization or other functions). Today, these specific functions are commonly called crosscutting concerns. Using the object-oriented approach, developers had a hard time implementing these crosscutting concerns seamlessly into their programs, because their nature prevented a clean separation of concerns and ultimately lead to

---

[1] See (Josupeit-Walter, 2008) or (Prechelt, 2001) for a summary of empirical research on object-orientation.
[2] Two papers which go into that direction are (Jones, 1994) and the follow-up (Steidley, 1994)

tangled and difficult to read code (imagine an example where each method call that had to be logged for debugging purposes needed a separate logging statement which had to be inserted manually into the code). This code was also very tough to maintain and change, as the calls to these functions were scattered across the rest of the code and one central code change to solve the problem (which is usually one of the main benefits of object-orientation, the encapsulation of functionality) was not possible. All these drawbacks lead to the idea of aspect-oriented programming, where the so called aspects replace the tangled and scattered fragments in the old code by one central isolated point, effectively modularizing the crosscutting concern in the code. For the logging example, this aspect could be given the task of calling the logging functionality (which might be a method of a class providing this function) on all occasions the developer wants it to. This makes it easy for the developer to have every single method call in the program be logged without having to insert logging statements into the code to log itself.

3.2.2. AspectJ – a short Introduction

AspectJ[1] is the implementation of the aspect-oriented add-on for the well-known and widely used programming language Java. It provides language constructs and mechanisms that implement the aspect-oriented crosscutting concerns using aspects. The paper (Kiczales, et al., 2001) presents an overview of AspectJ and its constructs, as well as how to use them. Some of these mechanisms will be explained here, but for a deeper introduction, the AspectJ Tutorial of the AspectJ project team[2] provides a more sophisticated resource.

AspectJ introduces the aspect language construct into Java, which is defined in practically the same way as a standard Java class and provides the language unit which encapsulates and modularizes crosscutting functionality. Kiczales and his colleagues differentiate the crosscutting mechanisms of AspectJ into dynamic crosscutting, meaning being able to run additional code at well-defined points during program execution, and static crosscutting, meaning the extension of existing types through new operations[3]. There is some confusion concerning the meaning of the terms dynamic and static crosscutting, as some seem to use these terms in different contexts for different concepts, others use them the way Kiczales and his colleagues did. So it cannot be clearly stated whether these definitions of dynamic and static crosscutting are deprecated today. For reasons of simplicity, this AspectJ

---

[1] As of the time of this work, AspectJ was available as version 1.6.2
[2] Their web site can be found at http://www.eclipse.org/aspectj/
[3] (Kiczales, et al., 2001), p.3

introduction focuses on the concepts which were originally meant by the notion of dynamic crosscutting: Running aspect code at well-defined points in the program.[1]

These well-defined points are commonly called join points and can represent different occasions during program execution, like a method call, an exception being thrown or the reading of a class field. A set of join points is called a pointcut (like all method calls in a certain class). Another interpretation might be to say that a join point is an incarnation of a certain pointcut definition, somehow like the relation of an object to a class. The code that is to be executed on the execution of a pointcut is called advice. The following code example shows the different concepts and their syntax in AspectJ:

```
package mypackage;

public aspect ExampleAspect {
      private boolean isvalid;

      private void setValid() {
            isvalid = true;
      }

      pointcut methodCall() :
            call(public String MyClass.*(..));

      before() : methodCall() {
            System.out.println "A method is called");
      }
}
```

Listing 3-1 – An example aspect in AspectJ Syntax

On a first look, the syntax of the aspect frame does not differ much from that of a class: It has a name, a package, can have imports and is defined the same as a class (it also gets its own source file), except for the keyword aspect that is used. An aspect can also have fields and methods, like the aspect from the example. These are the similarities between an aspect and a class, but more interesting are the aspect specific constructs: There is a pointcut definition called methodCall, which hooks itself onto all calls to public methods of the class MyClass which return a String. The method name, number of parameters and the parameter types are not relevant for this pointcut, as wildcards are used for the definition. Pointcuts use constructs called primitives, which represent certain points in program execution, like the call of a method (in the example, the call primitive is used). These wildcards and primitives make AspectJ a very powerful tool, interested readers should refer to the AspectJ documentation for more on wildcards and primitives as well as more AspectJ syntax. Hence, the pointcut stands for a set of join points in the program, specifically all occasions of calls to methods which return a String in the class MyClass. The last construct in

---

[1] (Hanenberg, 2005) provides a thorough description of dynamic and static features.

the example is the advice, which represents the code to be executed on certain occasions. In this case, a line is printed to the console every time before a method which fulfills the primitive of the `methodCall` pointcut is executed, indicated by the before keyword. Another possibility would be to use the after or around keywords, which can run the advice code after or instead of the original method call.

The process of putting together the object-oriented and aspect-oriented code is called weaving, where the weaver-process inserts the connection to the aspect advice code at the designated join points. This definition of weaving is rather rudimentary, but shall suffice in the context of this work, as a more exact description and explanation can be found in (Hanenberg, 2005), which is generally a good source of information on aspect-orientation concepts and background.

4. The Experiment

4.1.Experiment Buildup

4.1.1. The planned Course of the Experiment

The experiment in question was planned as a group of small sized programming tasks for the participants, consisting of two main assignments which each consisted of the same nine tasks. The nine tasks were designed so that each of them had different variables to influence their editing, which are described separately for each task below. Each of these assignments had to be fulfilled using the plain object-oriented approach (as the control language) as well as using only an aspect to solve the same problems. This means all participants had to do all nine tasks twice, some started with the object-oriented assignment, some with the aspect-oriented and then, after finishing, had to solve the same nine tasks using the other technique. It was randomly chosen who had to start with which assignment, but it was made sure that an even number of participants started with each. When using object-oriented programming, they were not allowed to use an aspect and while using aspect-oriented programming, they were not allowed to modify the original code and were permitted to modify their aspect only. The object-oriented tasks could only be solved by writing heavily redundant code, as can be seen in the descriptions of the specific tasks below. All participants, no matter which assignment they were given first, took part in a short AspectJ Tutorial of about 60-90 minutes in which they could try out some example exercises to get used to AspectJ syntax and handling. The tutorial concentrated only on a practical introduction to these parts and concepts of AspectJ which were needed to solve the tasks in the study while completely ignoring all remaining concepts of AspectJ. All in all, the experiment was planned to take each participant approximately 5 hours to complete, but no hard time limit was set.

4.1.2. The Questionnaire

Before beginning the study, all participants had to fill out an electronic questionnaire where they had to self-assess their skills and experience through various questions, mostly on a range from one to six. It included questions about general programming skills, Java, Eclipse or AspectJ experience and furthermore contained open slots for the participants to fill in any additional experience they had with different programming languages or techniques like logical programming. The data from the questionnaire was meant to be used later when trying to find out if specific previous knowledge influenced the participants' progress in the study. The whole original questionnaire can be found in the appendix.

4.1.3. The Hard- and Software used in the Experiment

4.1.3.1. The Application used for Editing

A self-written game designed explicitly for the experiment was used as the target application the participants had to work on, consisting of nine classes within three packages with 110 methods, eight constructors, and 37 instance variables written in pure Java (version 1.6). Each class was specified in its own file. The game has a small graphical user interface with an underlying event-based model-view-controller[1] architecture (see Figure 4-1) and was modified in large parts to fit the experiments requirements.

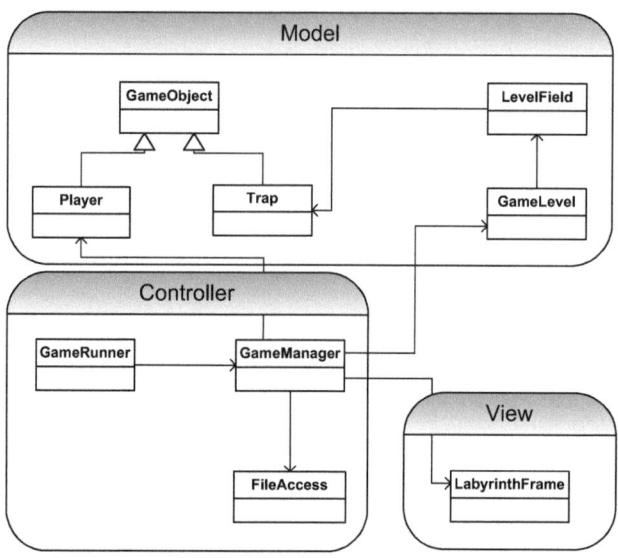

Figure 4-1 – A simplified UML Diagram of the target application

Essentially, the application is a simple text-based labyrinth game, where the player navigates through a labyrinth, walking towards the goal field while trying to avoid traps which are hidden on some fields. It has a JFrame called LabyrinthFrame, which acts as the view in the model-view-controller architecture and which is responsible for every type of feedback the user gets. Its registered listener for all events and actions is the GameManager class, which also acts as the core of the game, where the main game logic is controlled. The GameManager is called by the GameRunner class, which owns the main method and uses the FileAccess class, which provides

---

[1] More information on the Model-View-Controller design pattern can be found here:
http://en.wikipedia.org/wiki/Model-view-controller

functionality for reading level data from files. The GameObject, Player, Trap, GameLevel and LevelField classes represent the underlying model of the game.

4.1.3.2.   The Development Environment and Hardware

A set of Lenovo Thinkpad[1] laptops was used as computers for the study and every participant was provided with a mouse to make the most efficient programming possible. All had the same configuration, which consisted of the integrated development environment and the task workspaces, the batch files for starting the tasks (which were used to make starting eclipse using different workspaces easier), a database[2] for the data to be automatically logged during the experiment and a screen logging software[3].

As an integrated development environment, Eclipse Ganymede[4] was used, along with the AspectJ Development Tools plugin[5]. For logging reasons, a self-written development trace plugin (which is the detailed topic of the following work: (Josupeit-Walter, 2009)) had been added to Eclipse, which wrote the current workspace status into a database every time the user made a short break in editing the code (about two seconds of inactivity were needed to trigger it), saved the workspace or ran a test case. That way, a large base of data for evaluation could be generated for every task every participant had edited. Additionally, the screen logger installed on each computer was started before the participants began working on the tasks. Its videos were used for data redundancy purposes and to give additional data and detailed evaluation should the data in the database not be enlightening enough to reconstruct what a participant did.

These additional programs, especially the latency of eclipse that was induced by the regular workspace saving created some adverse conditions for the participants, as performance and reaction time of the Eclipse environment were significantly decreased during the experiment and the mouse pointer was flickering due to the screen logger. But as this was the case for every participant, the odds were still even and the effect applies to all data.

4.1.4. The Tasks

All tasks given to the participants had to be done in the order given to them. They received some sheets of paper which had the problem descriptions and instructions for each task on them, along with some general hints. Each task was started using a named batch file, which itself started Eclipse using the specific workspace for that task. The corresponding workspaces for each task also

---

[1] Specifically, they were R60's
[2] The database server was PostgreSQL in version 8.3: http://www.postgresql.org/
[3] CamStudio Version 2.00: http://camstudio.org/
[4] Which is Eclipse version 3.4 and can be found on http://www.eclipse.org
[5] Version 1.6.0 of the AJDT was used: http://www.eclipse.org/ajdt/

contained a set of test cases[1] the participants were instructed to use to evaluate their progress on the current task. That way they had the possibility to find out whether they were done with the current task and where they still had errors or unfinished work. Only if all test cases succeeded they were allowed to begin the next task. After each task, Eclipse had to be closed and the following task started using the next batch file. The first three larger tasks were supposed to provide an easy means of achieving better results using aspect-orientation, while for the smaller tasks it was predictable that plain object-orientation would generally achieve better results.

In the following chapters, all nine tasks are explained in more detail:

4.1.4.1.   Task1: The Logging Task

The first (and also the largest) task of the study was to add a logging-feature to the application, where each method (but no constructors) had to be supplemented with a call to the logger at the beginning of the method. For this, a corresponding logger-interface was provided which expected the name of the class where the method was declared in, the method name, the return type, an array of its actual parameter instances and an array of type String with the formal parameter names. An example for a log call is given below in Listing 4-1.

```
class C {
    public R m(int i, A a) {
        Logger.log("C", "m", "R",
            new Object[] {i, a},
            new String[] {"int", "A"} );

        //...method body...
    }
}
```

Listing 4-1 – An example statement of the Logging Task using only object-oriented programming

For a public method m in class C with parameter types int and A (and the corresponding parameter names i and a) and the return type R the corresponding invocation of the logger in pure Java that needed to be defined by the developer looks like shown above. The expected type names are simple names, i.e. no package names were expected by the logger. The consumed time by this task consists of the time for navigating to the right position in the code and writing the corresponding piece of code. Typically, developers do this via copy and paste, where they copy a previous logger-call and then copy the corresponding data into it. The object-oriented solution to this task was a very repetitive procedure, as the log statement had to be written or copied and modified for every method, making up 110 statements to create altogether. It can be assumed that the required time also depends on the number of parameters for each method, because for each parameter two

---

[1] Which were written for JUnit, a tool for running test cases: http://www.junit.org/

changed entries (compared to a previous log-invocation) needed to be specified (one for the parameter type and one for the actual parameter), which makes this a potential variable on the performance, even if its impact may be small. Within the 110 methods there were 45 without parameters, 39 with one parameter, 20 with two parameters, one with three parameters, four with four parameters and one with seven parameters.

The same task had to be solved in AspectJ, too. Thereto, the aspect definition, consisting of the keyword `aspect`, an aspect name and the corresponding brackets were given to the participant.

A good (and short) AspectJ solution for this task was to specify a pointcut that refers to the target classes via their package descriptions and a corresponding advice that reads the method signature and the actual parameters from `thisJoinPoint`. An example for such a piece of code that needed to be specified by each participant is shown in Listing 4-2.

```
pointcut logging():

     execution(* game.*.*(..)) ||
     execution(* filesystem.*.*(..)) ||
     execution(* gui.*.*(..));

before(): logging() {
     MethodSignature m = (MethodSignature) thisJoinPoint.getSignature();

     Class<?>[] classes = signature.getParameterTypes();

     String [] paramstrings = new String[classes.length];
     for (int i = 0; i < paramstrings.length; i++) {
          paramstrings[i] = classes[i].getSimpleName();
     }

     Logger.log(
          m.getDeclaringType().getSimpleName(),
          m.getName(),
          m.getReturnType().getSimpleName(),
          thisJoinPoint.getArgs(),
          paramstrings
     );
}
```

Listing 4-2 – A possible AspectJ Solution for the Logging Task

The participants did not get any hints about how to specify this aspect. Hence, this piece of code required some creative reasoning about AspectJ: The participants needed to think about how to use the language constructs of AspectJ in this situation. As a consequence, large variations of this piece of code were probable.

4.1.4.2. Task2: The Parameter Null Task

The second task was to add null reference-checks to all non-primitive parameters of all methods in the application (without constructors), which included strings and enumerations instances. In case one of the non-primitive parameters was null, an InvalidGameStateException should be thrown (which was part of the application and supplied in a separate package). For a method m in class C with parameter types int, A and B (and the corresponding parameter names i, a and b) the corresponding null-reference check that needed to be defined by the developer looks like shown in Listing 4-3.

```
class C {
    public R m(int i,A a, B b) {
        if(a == null || b == null)
            throw new InvalidGameStateException()
        //...method body...
    }
}
```

Listing 4-3 – The null-reference check using pure object-orientation

Altogether, 34 methods needed to be adapted. Similar to the first task, it can be assumed that the required time also depends on the variable number of non-primitive parameter types (in addition to the time required for typing the code for the first time), because even with copy and paste, the parameters still had to be renamed, added or removed. Within the 34 methods there were 29 methods with one, four methods with two and one with three non-primitive parameter types.

Again, in order to specify a corresponding aspect, a template for this aspect (without pointcut and advice) was given. In fact, a good solution could have the same pointcut as the one from the log-task. Within the corresponding advice it seems reasonable to reflect on the method's parameter types via the signature passed by thisJoinPoint (see Listing 4-4).

```
pointcut nullreferenceCheck():
    execution(* game.*.*(..)) ||
    execution(* filesystem.*.*(..)) ||
    execution(* gui.*.*(..));

before(): nullreferenceCheck () {
    MethodSignature m = (MethodSignature) thisJoinPoint.getSignature();

    for(int i=0; i < m.getParameterTypes(); i++) {
        if(!m.getParameterTypes()[i].isPrimitive
            && m.getArgs()[i] == null)
            throw new InvalidGameStateException();
    }
}
```

Listing 4-4 – A possible AspectJ solution for the null-reference checks

Again, the participants did not get any hint about how to implement the corresponding aspect. Consequently, a large variety of different implementations among the participants is probable. For example, AspectJ solutions which did not differ between primitive and reference types were perfectly valid, as primitive types could not have been null anyway.

4.1.4.3. Task3: The Synchronization Task

The third task was to add synchronization code to all methods within the three classes GameObject, Player, Trap and GameLevel. Thereto, the participants were explicitly asked to make use of the synchronize block provided by Java for which the task description already contained a template as shown in Listing 4-5. Altogether, 52 methods needed to be adapted by the participants.

```
class GameObject {

    public R m(int i, A a) {
        synchronized(this) {
            //...method body...
        }
    }
}
```
Listing 4-5 – The code template for the synchronization task

In contrast to the previous tasks it was not necessary to modify the inserted code, while in the previous examples some parameters, etc. had to be added, removed or modified, this code comes "as is". Nevertheless, a difference is that it is still no plain copy & paste approach: the participant has to navigate to the beginning of a method to add the synchronized-phrase as well as to the end of a method in order to insert the closing bracket. From that perspective, the length of the method might be an influencing variable factor on the time required to fulfill this task. However, the method length in our example application always fit on the display. Consequently, the influence of method length is considered not to be substantial and is neglected in further discussions.

```
pointcut syncs(Object o):
(
    execution(* GameObject.*(..)) ||
    execution(* Player.*(..)) ||
    execution(* Trap.*(..)) ||
    execution(* GameLevel.*(..));
) && this(o)

Object around(Object o): syncs(o) {
    synchronized(o) {
        return proceed();
    }
}
```
Listing 4-6 – The AspectJ solution for the synchronization task

For specifying the AspectJ version of this task, the participants needed to be familiar with the around and proceed language constructs of AspectJ. In contrast to the previous tasks there are not that many reasonable alternative solutions. The only possible differences manifest in whether the target object reference is being exposed by the pointcut definition (like specified in Listing 4-6) or whether thisJoinPoint is being used for this purpose.

4.1.4.4. Task4: The Check Player Argument Task

After the first three tasks, which consumed the largest part of the time, the check player task was a very short one. The GameManager class has four update methods which take a Player object as an argument. The task was to check for each update method whether this argument equals the Player object instance that the current GameManager references via its player attribute. If the instances would not match, an InvalidGameStateException had to be thrown. An example code excerpt is shown in Listing 3-1 below.

```
public void updatePlayer(Player playerarg) {
    if (playerarg != player)
        throw new InvalidGameStateException();

    //...method body
}
```

Listing 4-7 – An example object-oriented solution for the check player argument task

Because there are only four methods that had to be edited, this task was easy to do. The only variable in its editing could have been the time needed to find the four methods in the GameManager class, the code itself could be written the first time and copied for the other three times. But still, the approach could vary. This task was one of the tasks where the object-oriented approach was assumed to take much less time, because of the small number of methods to be edited.

Using AspectJ, the trick was to get a reference to the instance of the GameManager class which held the player attribute that had to be compared via this or target and use either context binding via the AspectJ args construct or the getArgs method of thisJoinPoint to get hold of a reference to the Player argument. A rough example solution could have looked like the following:

```
pointcut update(GameManager g) :
    execution(* GameManager.update*(..)) &&
    this(g);

before(GameManager g) : update(g) {
    if(g.player != thisJoinPoint.getArgs()[0])
        throw new InvalidGameStateException();
}
```

Listing 4-8 – Possible AspectJ solution for the check player argument task

A more elegant approach would have been the usage of the args keyword to bind the Player argument. But again, the pointcut and advice definitions could vary between all participants and still be legitimate solutions which solved the task.

4.1.4.5.   Task5: The Notify Observers Task

Fifth task among the nine was the notify observers task, where the participants had to insert a call to the `notifyObservers` method of the `GameObject` and `Player` classes each time an instance variable of these classes was set in one of their methods. This had to happen every time an instance variable was set, not just at the end of the method were the setting had happened. This made sure that even in methods where more than one variable was set the call to `notifyObservers` was done the according number of times, too (an example is shown below). All in all, 19 methods were subject of such editing.

```
public void setValues(int value1, int value2) {
    x = value1;
    notifyObservers();

    y = value2;
    notifyObservers();
}
```
Listing 4-9 – An object-oriented example for the notify observers task

The time needed for this task was influenced by the variables of the time for finding all set appearances of instance variables in the methods. The `notifyObservers` call could be copied into the code once it was written manually for the first time or could be written each time using the help of the Eclipse auto-completion feature.

One of the reasons for this approach was to keep the semantics the same as those from the AspectJ solution which had to be used for the task. Again, different solutions were possible. The following code shows a pointcut which made use of the fact that `Player` was a subclass of `GameObject` and binds the current instance via `this`.

```
pointcut Notify(GameObject g)  :
    set(* GameObject+.*) &&
    this(g);

after(GameObject g) : Notify (g) {
    g.notifyObservers();
}
```
Listing 4-10 – An AspectJ solution for the notify observers task

The above AspectJ construct makes sure that the `notifyObservers` method is called every time an instance variable of `GameObject` or `Player` is set, just like the task description specifies. With enough understanding of the AspectJ mechanics, it was possible to finish this task quite fast, even if the pure copy and paste approach of the object-orientation was very fast and easy to do itself, either.

4.1.4.6. Task6: The Observers Null Check Task

Immediately after the notify observers task the observers null check task had to be done. It was meant to complement the notify observers task, because now the participants had to add a null reference check before the call of the `notifyObservers` method in the classes `GameObject` and `Player` to make sure their `observers` list was not null. 15 methods had to be edited that way. When taking the example from above, a code sample could look like the following:

```
public void setValues(int value1, int value2) {
    x = value1;
    if (observers == null)
        throw new InvalidGameStateException();
    notifyObservers();

    y = value2;
    if (observers == null)
        throw new InvalidGameStateException();
    notifyObservers();
}
```
Listing 4-11 - An object-oriented example for the observers null check task

As can be seen, the semantics were kept the same as the previous task, originating from the same cause of keeping them close to those of the aspect, requiring a null check before each call to `notifyObservers`. The time needed for this task was, like the previous task, influenced by the variables of the time for finding all `notifyObservers` calls in the code (which should have been a little easier now, as the participants already edited the same code parts in the previous task). Again, after writing the necessary code once, it could be copied and pasted for all other times.

A possible solution of the task via AspectJ is shown below.

```
pointcut ObserversCheck(GameObject o) :
    call (void GameObject+.notifyObservers(..)) &&
    target(o);

before(GameObject o) : ObserversCheck (o) {
    if(o.observers == null) throw new InvalidGameStateException();
}
```
Listing 4-12 - An AspectJ solution for the observers null check task

The pointcut definition could be kept simple, as only the calls to the `notifyObservers` method needed to be captured and it was sufficient to make a null reference check on the `observers` instance variable of the object in the advice. Different solutions were possible, like using explicit pointcut definitions for the two classes or the `execution` primitive along with `this`.

4.1.4.7.   Task7: The Refresh Constraint Task

Task number seven is called the refresh constraint task, where the goal is to check integer values which are passed to all methods of the `LabyrinthFrame` class whose names begin with refresh. Those methods are responsible for passing these integer values on to `JLabel` fields which present these values to the user. These integer values have to be checked whether they are of a value smaller than (-1), which would be an invalid value and therefore an `InvalidGameStateException` should be thrown in the case. Listing 4-13 demonstrates an example.

```
public void refreshValue(int value) {
      if(value < -1)
            throw new InvalidGameStateException();
      //..methody body
}
```

Listing 4-13 –Possible solution for the refresh constraint task using object-orientation

Participants only had to write the if-statement once and could copy it for the next time. A possible variable could be the number of parameters the methods had, where participants had to use an or-clause or copy and edit two if-statements to fulfill the task. Altogether, eight methods had to be edited with these refresh constraints.

Aspects that fulfilled this task were a bit trickier, because of the boxing[1] behavior in Java. Either the participants avoided the unboxing procedure by using different pointcuts, where the args primitive removed the need to unbox the integer values, or they used the `getArgs` method and unboxed the values for checking, as is shown in the aspect example below:

```
pointcut refreshes() :
      execution(* LabyrinthFrame.refresh*(..));

before () : refreshes() {
      for (int i = 0; i < thisJoinPoint.getArgs().length; i++) {
            if (((Integer)thisJoinPoint.getArgs()[i]).intValue() < -1)
                  throw new InvalidGameStateException();
      }
}
```

Listing 4-14 - An AspectJ solution for the refresh constraint task

The aspect attaches itself to all methods of `LabyrinthFrame` starting with refresh, uses the `getArgs` method to obtain the arguments, unboxes the values and does the check. As can be seen, the code for unboxing the integer values out of the `Object` array references looks rather ugly. The `Object` has to be cast to the type `Integer` (which is the so called wrapper class for integer

---

[1] Encapsulating a primitive value type (like integer) into a reference type (for example of type `Object` or its corresponding wrapper class `Integer`) is called boxing, where the primitive value of the integer is moved to the heap and replaced by a reference to it on the stack.

values), and after this, the intValue method has to be used to acquire the real primitive integer value which is boxed in the Integer type object. Because the fact that this code is ugly and such occurrences of boxing and unboxing do not appear in the day to day tasks of developers too often, many participants possibly would not have known how to write the code for the unboxing procedure. To eliminate this large factor, which would possibly have consumed a lot of time and made the code more error prone, a small hint was given in the tasks description along with a code sample on how to use unboxing. With this hint, this variable should have been eliminated.

4.1.4.8. Task8: The Label Value Check Task

Penultimate among the tasks was task eight, the label value check task. During this task, the participants had to write code which checks the value of a JLabel for correctness just after it is set. Essentially, it was only needed to call the getText method of the JLabel and check its returned string for correctness. Correctness was defined as a number between zero and nine or an empty string as the last character. Participants were not required to write the code which performed the real string check themselves, they were rather provided with a convenience method called isValidLabelString, which performed the check and returned true or false. On return of a false, an InvalidGameStateException had to be thrown. Ultimately, the only code fragments that needed to be written were like the following:

```
public void refreshLabelString(String text) {
    //...method body

    if(!isValidLabelString(mylabel.getText()))
        throw new InvalidGameStateException();
}
```

Listing 4-15 - Possible solution for the label value check task using object-orientation

Such a code fragment had to be inserted into six methods altogether. This time there were practically no variables, as the code could be copied and pasted and only the name of the label had to be altered in the if-statement.

In contrast to the object-oriented solution, the aspects that fulfilled this task where probably the hardest to write of all nine tasks. Participants needed to get a reference to either the instance of the LabyrinthFrame object (to be able to call the isValidLabelString method, which is not static) and the reference to the JLabel whose text had been set.

```
pointcut afterSetText(JLabel label, LabyrinthFrame f):
    call(* JLabel.setText(..)) &&
    this(f) &&
    target(label);
```

```
after(JLabel j, LabyrinthFrame f) : afterSetText(j, f) {
    if(!f.isValidLabelString(j.getText()))
        throw new InvalidGameStateException();
}
```

Listing 4-16 - An AspectJ solution for the label value check task

This aspect probably required the most thinking and trickiest use of AspectJ. Just getting the string argument for the refresh method was not sufficient to fulfill this task, as it was important that the check happened after the call to the setText method of the label. The participants needed to have understood the concepts of both the this and target primitives. Another approach would have been to create a new LabyrinthFrame instance just to get access to the isValidLabelString method, so that only the JLabel reference would have been needed to be acquired via pointcut.

4.1.4.9.   Task9: The Current Level Check Task

The last task to be done was the current level check task. Goal of the task was to check whether the level boundaries of a new level which was loaded where greater than the boundaries of the current level. The point for the check was every time the currentlevel instance variable of the GameManager class was set in the program code. Participants did not have to write the check logic themselves, as a convenience method called checkLevelConstraints was provided for the task, which took the current and the new level as arguments and returned a true or a false. On return of a false, an InvalidGameStateException had to be thrown.

```
public void sampleMethod() {

    //...method body

    GameLevel newlevel = loadLevel(levelnumber);
    if (!checkLevelConstraints(newlevel, currentlevel))
        throw new InvalidGameStateException();
    currentlevel = newlevel;

    //...method body
}
```

Listing 4-17 - Possible solution for the current level check task using object-orientation

The object-oriented solution did not require much thinking and could be copied and pasted once a correct solution had been typed once. No adjustments had to be made in the code. The only variable was the time needed to search for the occurrences in the GameManager code where the currentlevel instance variable was set.

The aspect which solved this task needed to hook itself onto the setting of the currentlevel instance variable via the set primitive and get the reference to the GameManager instance via this (as the checkLevelConstraints method is not static).

```
pointcut setLevel(GameManager m) :
    set(public GameLevel GameManager.currentlevel) &&
    this(m);

before(GameManager m) : setLevel(m){
    if(m.currentlevel != null) {


        if(!m.checkLevelConstraints((GameLevel)thisJoinPoint.getArgs()[0],
            m.currentlevel))
            throw new InvalidGameStateException();
    }
}
```

Listing 4-18 - An AspectJ solution for the current level check task

The aspect needed to get the reference to the level to be set using the `getArgs` method and a cast to `GameLevel`. And it contained an additional pitfall, as the `currentlevel` variable could be null in specific situations in the program flow, which required a check against not null.

4.2.Implementation of the Experiment

The implementation of the experiment was started by a phase where possible participants were recruited using personal contact, e-mail newsletters and forums which are commonly frequented by computer science students and students of related sciences. As the participants were not paid anything for their participation and time consumption of the experiment was communicated as about 4-5 hours, feedback from possibly interested participants was relatively low. At the end of the implementation phase, 24 people had partaken in the experiment. Most of them were computer science or business information systems students, but also one software developer from the industry and a few university teachers.

The first difficulty after making contact was to find dates and times to which the participants had time to spare. It was impossible to get a group larger than two or three participants at a single time and day, which made the whole process of giving the tutorial, supervising the fulfillment of the tasks, saving data and videos and preparing the computer for the next participant a very time consuming one. The experiment implementation phase was planned to take two weeks at first, but had to be extended to nearly five weeks, because of the scheduling problems with all participants.

During the passes of the first participants, a problem with the original timing plan for the tasks revealed itself, as the time the development tracing tool added to the overall time had not been taken into account and now lead to an increased time needed to finish all the tasks. Additionally, most of the participants had large problems in solving the aspect-oriented tasks and it took them a lot longer than originally estimated. In the end, only a small group of participants stayed in the projected time limit of about four to five hours overall experiment time.

As another result of this huge time multiplication, the videos captured by the screen logger became very big, much bigger than assumed and some turned out to be partially corrupted because of that fact.

Another problem originated from some strange hang-ups the Eclipse environment sometimes suffered right after starting a new task, requiring the Eclipse GUI to be shutdown and restarted. This lead to the problem of multiple session ids for one task of some participants, as these session ids were generated and written into the database each time a participant started a new task. As a best case this meant that there existed exactly 18 session ids (9 aspect-oriented tasks, 9 object-oriented) for each participant after the experiment. Because of the crashes, which sometimes even happed while working on a task, for some participants multiple session ids were created for some tasks. This has lead to additional problems in the analysis phase.

Two of the participants did not manage to finish working on both task sets. Because of a lack of time, one only did the object-oriented part and one the aspect-oriented. The progress of two other participants was not saved into the database correctly because of a wrongly configured file for the development trace tool. All in all, 20 fully usable datasets were available after the experiment, along with one additional object-oriented dataset and one aspect-oriented from the two participants who could not bring up the time to finish all tasks.

5. Experiment Analysis and Results

Preparation and processing of the gathered data for later evaluation was started even while the experiment implementation phase was still running. The whole gathered data taken together formed a huge mass of information, which was way too overwhelming when only considering the goal of this experiment, as the development tracing tool was bound to save the complete workspace into the database every few seconds, along with a lot of additional data like keyboard input, shortcuts or eclipse commands. Description of the steps for data preparation, processing and analysis are only focused on the data relevant for this experiment.

5.1.Data Processing and Preparation

As the interest of this experiment was primarily to measure the successes per time (where successes being the number of fulfilled test cases) for each task and programming technique to possibly create a time series afterwards, it was important to only extract the data needed for that process from the database. First, a time interval had to be chosen at which the development tracing tool would extract the required data from the database, because extracting every so called snapshot of a workspace from the database would have taken a huge amount of time. As a first interval, 30 seconds were chosen. For the extraction procedure, the tool needed to be supplied with the requested time interval and the session id, which uniquely identified one eclipse session for one task of one user, as already stated above. A list was created manually which mapped the specific task and related programming technique to the corresponding session id or session ids (sometimes an Eclipse crash right in the middle of working on a task required more than one session to be provided to the tool for extraction of one tasks complete result). In some worst cases, the correct session ids could only be found out by looking into the screen captured videos and making a time stamp comparison between the video and the sessions in the database. After that, the tool was started via automatically created batch files for each of these sessions and extracted the required snapshots (a snapshot is a buildable version of the eclipse workspace of the corresponding task) from the database for the 30 seconds interval.

After the snapshots for the tasks were available, the tool needed to iterate over these snapshots, build each one and run all the test cases on each of these and write the results into the database, so that a "successes per time"-series could be created. To create even more fine-grained data, evaluation aspects were written which printed out additional data for each test case run into a stream which was written into the database along with the other data and the result of success or failure for the specific test case. Because errors which the compiled snapshots sometimes contained initially compromised this evaluation, resulting in faulty data, it was necessary to write additional pointcuts and advice into the evaluation aspects which encapsulated the invocation of the test case methods and made sure all exceptions were caught and did not harm the evaluation process. For the smaller tasks, it became necessary to use a smaller time interval of five seconds, because the 30 seconds interval that was initially chosen created too rough time series for these tasks.

For the aspect-oriented results, it soon became clear that no useful time lines could be created from them, as there was no real order apparent they were following. Most of them consisted just of many intervals where no successes were achieved at all, and the next 30 seconds lead to the complete success in all test cases. As this was the supposed and expected nature of the aspect results, the thought of creating time series diagrams for the aspect-oriented tasks had to be abandoned. Therefore, it was necessary to have at least a precise idea of what time was needed exactly for the aspect-oriented tasks, which is why a new database procedure was created, which used the data from the database to extract the exact number of seconds a participant required for one task in aspect-orientation. As a starting point, the first time a participant edited the workspace was chosen, as it was assumed that at this time the task description had been read and understood and working on the aspect had began. As the ending time, the first timestamp where all test cases for this task succeeded was taken. The difference between both was taken as the time needed for that task. As this approach seemed to generate precise results, it was taken to calculate the object-oriented overall editing time, too.

Because correlation values were below seventy percent on some result sets, a look into the corresponding video was taken (if available) and the possible source of the bad correlation (like taking a wrong approach and then correcting it, resulting in long time spans where no successes where generated) was noted along with the data. And because there were some inconsistencies in the data (manifesting in above mentioned bad correlation), like participants doing a short break which was not noticed, making a pause in thinking, etc. there was the idea of cleaning the data from these possible disturbances. So, a database procedure was written to remove all entries from a result set where the ratio of changed successes per time differed more than eighty percent from the average number of successes done in the complete time. The idea behind this was that while doing a redundant task in code over and over again, the average time for each success should be nearly identical when removing all disturbance factors like users taking a break or thinking. This breaks the data down to the raw editing of the code and pushes correlation even further, as can be seen from the cleansed data in the diagrams and tables shown later. This data cleansing could only be done for the larger tasks, as the smaller task results consisted of too few entries at all and too many were removed by the procedure, generating mostly unusable data.

The data from the questionnaire was also evaluated and used to try to categorize the participants depending on the answers they provided for each question. To be able to better create groups based on skill or experience profiles, the participants were asked an additional question regarding their overall experience with reflection techniques, which supposedly aided in solving the aspect-oriented tasks.

5.2.Data analysis and presentation

In this chapter, diagrams and aggregated data which form most of the results of the experiment are shown, split into chapters to display the data for each task separately[1]. Analysis starts with building time lines for the object-oriented approach, shown in diagrams and tables. For the first three tasks, the attempt to create cleansed time lines was also made, as can be seen later. A separate chapter contains an overall time analysis and some descriptive statistics as well as statistical tests and an additional chapter attempts to perform a break-even analysis using the object-oriented time lines and the aspect-oriented overall time needed for each task. Finally, it was tried to group the participants into skill groups and tested whether these groupings show significant results.

5.2.1. The Logging Task

Finally, after the necessary data had been written into the database, the required time series could be created from it.

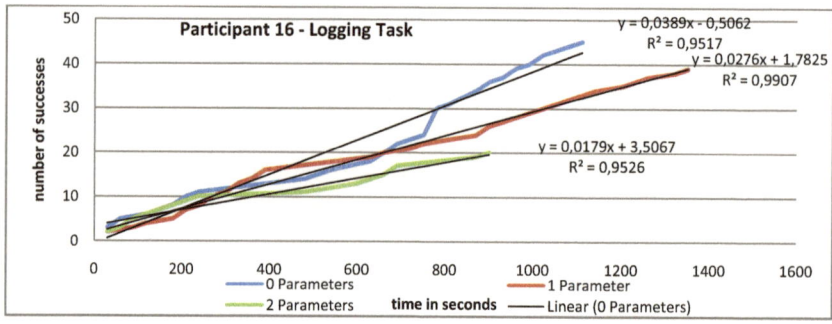

Figure 5-1 – A sample diagram showing progress per time in seconds depending on parameter count of methods for participant 16 and the Logging task

---

[1] Software used for the preparation, processing and presentation of the data was: SPSS Clementine 12, SPSS 16 and Microsoft Excel 2007

For the first task of Logging, the lines were also split according to the performance dependent on the number of parameters the methods had which had to be edited, along with the overall successes performance, as shown in the example diagrams below. To save space, the full diagrams are only shown for an example participant, and the resulting data has been aggregated into tables for all other participants. The upper diagram shows the progress of participant 16 for the Logging task, split into separate lines for methods with different numbers of parameters. Regression lines, their equations and the coefficients of determination (R^2) are shown, too. As methods with zero, one or two parameters made up the bulk of all methods and methods with more parameters were too rare to create useful lines from their success count, their counts are omitted here. On the y-axis, the number of successfully edited methods is represented (originating from fulfilled test cases) and the x-axis represents the time in seconds.

The lower diagram only shows the overall performance of participant 16 for the Logging Task along with a regression line laid through it. As can be seen from the line and the coefficient of determination, the measurement points seem to correlate nicely in an almost linear fashion for this participant and this task. A similar pair of diagrams was created for all other participants, too, but for the sake of space and clarity, their values are aggregated into the following table, so this chapter does not get crowded with diagrams. In all tables, the R^2 has been multiplied with 100% to save space. Most of the graphs have a similar form like the ones from the shown diagrams of participant 16, some with more or less larger dents and overall derivation from the regression line, but all in all similar. The constants for the regression equations have been rounded up the fourth decimal place.

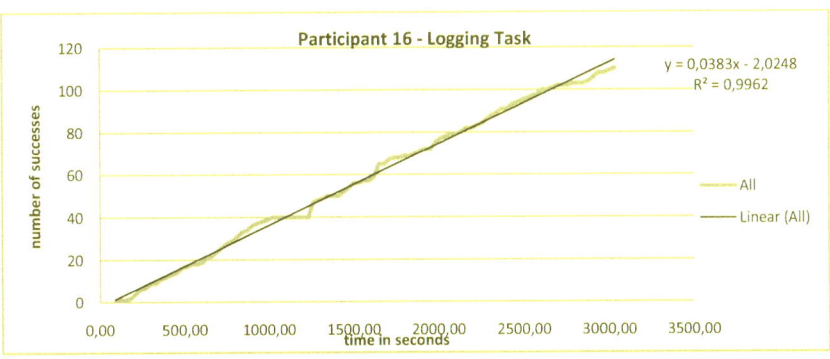

Figure 5-2 – A sample diagram showing overall unaltered progress of participant 16 on the Logging task

Variations in the time series can possibly be explained through the nature of the redundant task. Most code could be copied and pasted, with only a slight portion of it needing an adjusting. When changing from one class file to another, a slightly larger adjustment had to be made, along with the time consumed by opening the new file and perhaps getting an overview of it. To explain many larger dents in the curve, a full screening of the videos would need to be done, which is out of the scope of this work. A look into the videos was only taken if an R^2 value was lower than 70%, indicating a larger derivation, and explanations are given in the footnotes.

Nr.	0 Parameters		1 Parameter		2 Parameters		All	
	Equation	R^2	Equation	R^2	Equation	R^2	Equation	R^2
1	0,0213x - 6,1132	88,49%	0,0189x + 1,4413	98,21%	0,0113x + 1,1397	97,37%	0,0273x - 15,245	97,37%
2	0,02x + 2,1186	91,1%	0,0132x + 3,5318	98,14%	0,0106x + 2,3023	85,43%	0,0206x - 4,0422	97,61%
3	0,0426x - 3,5773	92,7%	0,0357x + 0,9243	98,55%	0,0268x + 0,5263	97,74%	0,0419x - 8,7842	98,68%
4	0,0089x - 1,1699	97,65%	0,0101x - 2,635	95,83%	0,0048x + 2,6312	97,77%	0,0149x - 24,908	94%
5	0,0194x - 2,3784	94,73%	0,0145x - 4,6431	94,32%	0,0221x - 2,1797	99,72%	0,0187x - 18,33	97,75%
6	0,0206x + 2,0139	88,07%	0,0156x + 1,385	97,59%	0,0137x - 1,0365	97,4%	0,0172x - 10,211	97,89%
7	0,0575x - 11,927	97,69%	0,035x - 18,563	94,66%	0,0156x - 4,8653	76,28%	0,0405x - 30,971	93,71%
8	0,0268x + 0,8379	96,72%	0,0182x + 2,3102	98,44%	0,0115x + 1,4229	97,5%	0,0259x - 22,775	98%
9	0,0176x - 5,0446	93,06%	0,0131x + 0,1489	98,34%	0,0092x + 0,2851	96,61%	0,027x - 11,18	97,45%
10	0,0317x - 5,0202	96,84%	0,0278x - 9,8083	82,45%	0,0301x - 17,574	91,51%	0,0567x - 39,903	94,59%
11	0,0225x - 0,7029	97,49%	0,0038x + 9,7254	81,89%	0,0096x + 3,4167	84,69%	0,0081x + 9,8202	82,79%
12	0,0353x - 3,2865	99,41%	0,0193x + 1,5771	98,21%	0,0223x - 0,9173	97,19%	0,0253x - 13,02	99,31%
13	0,0167x - 2,0229	97,52%	0,0097x + 2,2239	91,44%	0,0072x - 1,2855	87,97%	0,0175x - 11,997	45,93%[1]
14	0,0381x - 0,8989	98,75%	0,0326x - 0,1375	99,34%	0,0302x - 0,0075	99,06%	0,0345x - 9,9291	99,76%
15	0,0481x + 0,3899	98,35%	0,033x + 0,5152	99,78%	0,026x - 1,1264	98,68%	0,0434x - 8,6311	99,52%
16	0,0398x − 0,5062	95,17%	0,0276x + 1,7825	99,07%	0,0179x + 3,5067	95,26%	0,038x − 2,0248	99,62%
17	0,0251x + 0,0168	88,54%	0,0205x + 0,6683	95,21%	0,0122x + 0,5957	80,87%	0,0346x - 14,923	93,86%
18	0,0262x - 10,397	91,1%	0,0163x - 4,3212	94,17%	0,0264x - 1,2104	96,72%	0,0252x - 19,172	95,28%
19	0,0394x - 3,5711	96,53%	0,0291x - 3,8711	97,54%	0,0316x + 1,0104	96,28%	0,046x - 42,538	97,8%
20	0,0197x - 3,1204	98,2%	0,0205x - 3,029	98,37%	0,0152x - 2,3857	98,88%	0,0187x - 27,562	99,32%

Table 5-1 – Regression equations and determination coefficients for all participants for the Logging task using unaltered data

The next diagrams show the time lines for the Logging Task for participant 16 after removing any entries were the ratio of changed successes per time differed more than eighty percent from the average number of successes done in the complete time. The idea behind this was that while doing a redundant task in code over and over again, the average time for each success should be nearly identical, when removing all disturbance factors like users taking a break or thinking. This breaks the data down to the raw editing of the code and pushes correlation even further, as can be seen from the cleansed data in the diagrams and table below.

---

[1] Cause of bad correlation: exact source could not be found, but was possibly caused by the participant having syntax errors in the document preventing compilation from happening, resulting in very few overall measurement points.

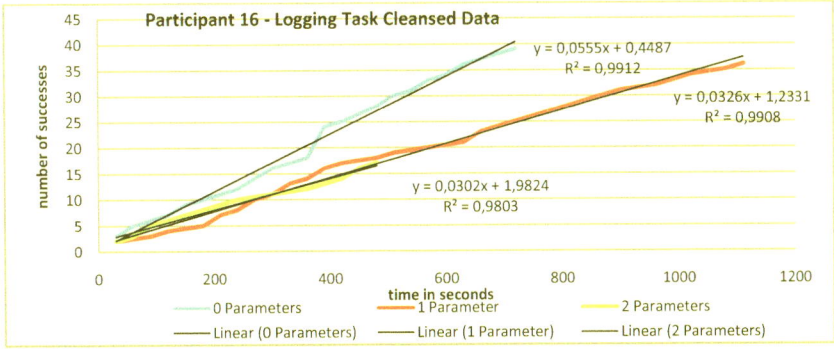

Figure 5-3 A sample diagram showing progress per time in seconds depending on parameter count of methods for participant 16 and the Logging task after data cleansing

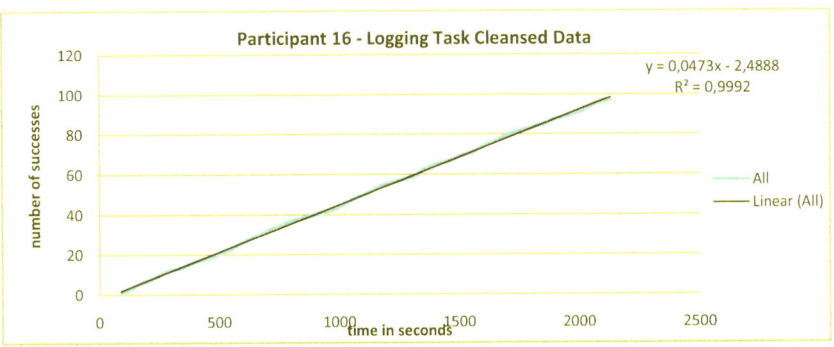

Figure 5-4 sample diagram showing overall unaltered progress of participant 16 on the Logging task after data cleansing

In the table below, all values for the cleansed data are shown for all participants. When comparing these with the values from the table above, it becomes clear that the correlation of the data has been improved significantly. Correlation is now very good in most cases; especially the correlation for all methods is extremely high now, as no value goes below 98 percent. This might be a strong hint showing that writing redundant code like in this task in plain object-oriented (or procedural) programming can be thought of as an almost linear function, perhaps making time predictions or other forecasts on the cost of redundant code possible.

Nr.	0 Parameters		1 Parameter		2 Parameters		All	
	Equation	R^2	Equation	R^2	Equation	R^2	Equation	R^2
1	0,0348x - 4,5437	98,7%	0,0205x + 1,1241	98,54%	0,0113x + 1,1397	97,37%	0,0431x - 15,896	99,78%
2	0,0358x - 1,3995	99,37%	0,0179x + 2,4874	98,86%	0,02x - 0,2396	98,94%	0,0405x - 8,4512	99,62%
3	0,0444x - 5,6319	98,19%	0,04x - 0,5052	99,56%	0,0312x + 0,8844	98,91%	0,0529x - 6,0862	99,85%
4	0,0219x - 10,147	98,48%	0,0108x - 2,7707	96,28%	0,006x + 1,7208	97,59%	0,0333x – 28	100%
5	0,0325x - 0,6447	99,24%	0,0287x - 3,3428	99,53%	0,0236x - 1,112	99,59%	0,0384x - 28,029	99,71%
6	0,0296x - 3,1507	99,41%	0,0189x + 0,6096	99,8%	0,0186x - 2,2494	99,45%	0,0381x - 22,388	99,86%
7	0,0512x - 4,76	98,72%	0,0385x - 18,464	98,06%	0,0358x - 2,6845	98,6%	0,0608x - 14,849	99,56%
8	0,0377x + 0,9784	99%	0,0221x + 1,6548	99,32%	0,0202x + 0,0585	94,44%	0,044x - 31,286	99,61%
9	0,015x - 0,8	98,19%	0,0181x + 0,0556	99,3%	0,0142x - 3,8532	86,12%	0,0468x - 8,2151	99,13%
10	0,034x - 5,5788	94,71%	0,0441x - 2,2519	97,78%	0,0319x - 17,194	97,8%	0,0894x - 36,144	98,87%
11	0,0359x - 0,8982	99,57%	0,012x + 1,5368	99,74%	0,0176x - 0,1553	99,05%	0,0333x – 63	100%
12	0,0423x - 3,1532	99,87%	0,0236x + 0,1229	99,64%	0,0265x - 0,7177	99,5%	0,0385x - 14,551	99,95%
13	0,0155x + 0,5436	99,99%	0,0157x + 1,2423	99,5%	0,0056x - 0,2399	98,65%	0,0326x - 12,756	98%
14	0,0436x - 1,3133	99,08%	0,0362x + 0,8489	99,47%	0,0372x + 0,3407	99,55%	0,0421x - 9,2237	99,9%
15	0,0574x - 1,1508	98,17%	0,0365x + 0,8903	99,88%	0,0308x - 2,4656	99,82%	0,0481x - 6,5903	99,52%
16	0,0555x + 0,4487	99,12%	0,0326x + 1,2331	99,08%	0,0302x + 1,9824	98,03%	0,0473x - 2,4888	99,92%
17	0,0504x - 1,3633	98,8%	0,0263x + 0,0008	99,67%	0,0307x - 1,2546	99,59%	0,0458x - 10,745	99,75%
18	0,035x - 4,3687	97,71%	0,0235x + 0,0963	97,95%	0,0259x - 1,5488	99,26%	0,0476x - 14,162	99,75%
19	0,0515x - 3,3161	99,18%	0,0345x + 1,5983	99,45%	0,0367x - 0,0542	99,54%	0,0627x - 45,084	99,38%
20	0,0267x - 5,0327	98,84%	0,0263x - 3,7541	98,97%	0,0177x - 3,4414	99,01%	0,0379x - 46,467	99,73%

Table 5-2 Regression equations and determination coefficients for all participants for the Logging task using cleansed data

5.2.2. The Parameter Null Task

As with the Logging task, it was first tried to split the analysis of object-oriented code progress into time lines depending on the number of parameters, but the methods with a parameter count larger than one were to rare to create useful lines from them, so this idea was omitted for this task. Its evaluation concentrates only on the overall progress.

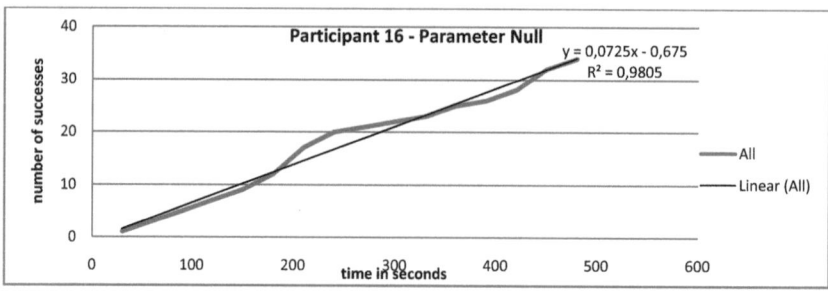

Figure 5-5 - A sample diagram showing overall unaltered progress of participant 16 on the Parameter Null task

Variations in this task's progress line could result from the time needed to examine the methods, find those with reference parameters, and adjust the code to check whether these are null. Below is the table with the aggregated data. Some participants erroneously inserted null checks into constructors, too (which was explicitly forbidden in the task description), resulting in some test cases not running correctly. This could be the source of the larger variations among the correlation values. This task also provided enough measurement data to make a data cleansing possible. The cleansed values are contained in the table in the rightmost columns.

Nr.	All			
	Equation	R^2	Equation cleansed	R^2 cleansed
1	0,0296x + 3,1541	86,06%	0,0593x - 6,0976	98,23%
2	0,0515x - 5,1966	96,42%	0,0648x - 5,6367	98,79%
3	0,0465x + 0,8604	94,01%	0,0693x - 1,1176	97,16%
4	0,0368x - 4,3892	96,63%	0,0537x - 6,6618	98,35%
5	0,0169x + 5,7437	82,54%	0,0446x - 2,8701	99,37%
6	0,0319x - 6,8326	97,78%	0,05x - 11,715	99,53%
7	0,0488x + 0,851	86,17%	0,0906x - 10,618	98,97%
8	0,0177x + 11,253	66,91%[1]	0,066x - 8,7298	99,12%
9	0,0325x - 8,5592	72,05%[2]	0,0648x - 3,019	95,27%
10	0,0521x - 6,0138	95,06%	0,0745x - 4,6588	97,85%
11	0,0407x - 5,8484	96,56%	0,0575x - 6,4489	98,59%
12	0,0225x - 0,4936	83,37%	0,0421x - 11,806	99,63%
13	0,0695x - 19,768	92,16%	0,0617x - 15,554	69,51%
14	0,0451x - 3,2923	98,14%	0,0543x - 5,7645	99,16%
15	0,0721x - 0,2119	93,09%	0,1135x - 4,9394	99,33%
16	0,0725x - 0,675	98,05%	0,0921x - 3,1212	99,04%
17	0,0613x - 3,4641	96,76%	0,0757x - 2,3971	97,59%
18	0,0569x - 5,4376	97,55%	0,0655x - 3,3068	98,16%
19	0,082x - 8,7516	98,78%	0,1093x - 11,57	99,2%
20	0,0355x - 8,3132	97,29%	0,0454x - 6,8278	99,39%

Table 5-3 - Regression equations and determination coefficients for all participants for the Parameter Null task using unaltered data and cleansed data

5.2.3. The Synchronization Task

Task number three was only evaluated for the number of successes and overall performance; no extra fine-grained comparisons were done, like the splitting into parameter numbers of the Logging Task. Below is another a sample diagram of participant 16, showing the overall progress on the task, the following table again shows all aggregated data. Depending on the approach the participants would take for this task, most variations in progress seem to come from the fact that the participants had to insert the synchronized block header at the beginning of the method and had to search for the end of the method to insert the closing bracket. Switching to the next class file also has to be

---

[1] Cause of bad correlation: Participant had edited constructors with null checks by mistake, resulting in some test cases not running correctly. The participant needed a larger amount of time to discover and correct that mistake, resulting in a stretched line with worse correlation than average.

[2] Even if this participant did not have a correlation below 70%, a random scan of the video showed that he inserted null checks for parameters of value types, too. This fact explains the smaller correlation value.

taken into account. As with the first two tasks, the Synchronized task contained enough measurement points to make a data cleansing possible without completely rendering many time lines useless. The cleansed values are shown in the table below. Again, similar to the phenomenon on the first two tasks, correlation improves considerably through data cleansing, strengthening the idea that redundant code progress develops in a linear fashion.

Nr.	All			
	Equation	R^2	Equation cleansed	R^2 cleansed
1	0,122x - 12,9	97,81%	0,1524x - 14,127	98,69%
2	0,1056x - 13,089	83,7%	0,1064x - 4,5	99,61%
3	0,1195x - 6,8199	94,74%	0,2679x - 6,4286	96,62%
4	0,0323x - 3,2214	85,63%	0,0928x - 3,3399	98,59%
5	0,0723x - 13,688	97,84%	0,0997x - 21,088	98,67%
6	0,0486x - 12,502	80,01%	0,0889x - 5,8617	97,93%
7	0,1226x - 4,887	95,15%	0,1694x + 1,5909	98,77%
8	0,1327x - 4,5824	95,18%	0,2524x – 3	98,15%
9	0,0979x - 12,185	57,01%[1]	0,2667x – 7	100%
10	0,1207x - 7,9714	87,31%	0,2x – 6	92,31%
11	0,0937x - 9,8316	98,33%	0,1079x - 6,6238	99,34%
12	0,0697x - 0,3394	97,46%	0,1044x + 6,2574	99,49%
13	0,1049x - 6,6948	44,47%[2]	0,2667x + 2	100%
14	0,1088x - 5,7647	96,4%	0,1459x - 9,1655	98,2%
15	0,1324x - 8,4852	78,8%	0,2x + 1,6667	96,43%
16	0,1127x - 4,3603	98,56%	0,1464x + 2,2	98,79%
17	0,1391x - 5,4044	97,63%	0,1786x - 10,424	98,57%
18	0,1195x - 6,8199	94,74%	0,1917x - 5,1944	98,98%
19	0,1037x - 10,235	94,67%	0,2267x - 6,8	92,26%
20	0,0588x - 5,4793	98,99%	0,0734x - 1,7935	99,77%

Table 5-4 - Regression equations and determination coefficients for all participants for the Synchronization task using unaltered data and cleansed data

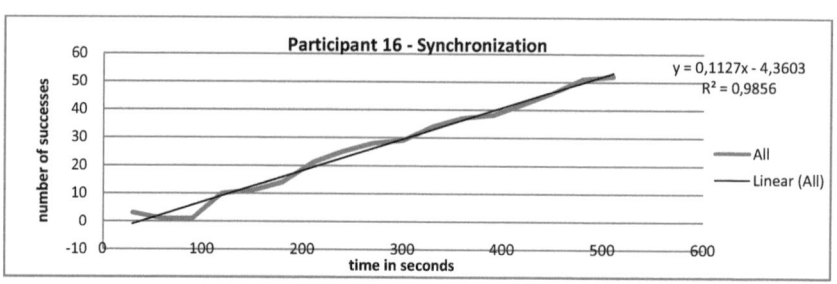

Figure 5-6 - A sample diagram showing overall unaltered progress of participant 16 on the Synchronization task

---

[1] Cause of bad correlation: Participant had used an approach where he first inserted all synchronize block headers for all methods, and added the closing brackets for all methods after that.
[2] Cause of bad correlation: Participant did not use synchronize blocks as the task description said, but only set each whole method synchronized, saving a lot of time and generating very few measurement points.

5.2.4. The Player Check Task

The Player Check task was one of the smaller tasks, requiring measurement intervals of five seconds for each point. Apart from that, evaluation did not differ much from the larger tasks. It was also the smallest of all tasks with only four test cases to fulfill all in all.

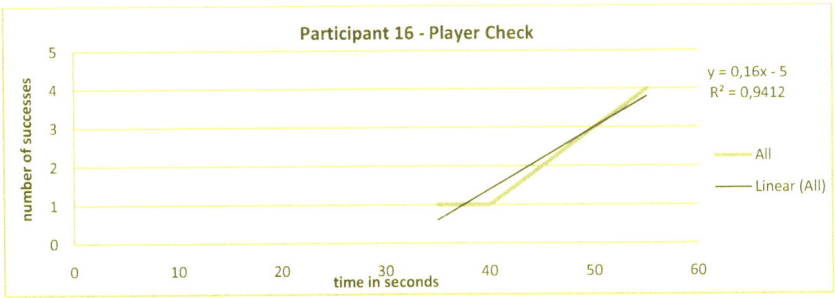

Figure 5-7 - A sample diagram showing overall unaltered progress of participant 16 on the Player Check task

Nr.	All	
	Equation	R^2
1	$0,16x - 13,6$	88,89%
2	$0,2x - 13,5$	83,33%
3	$0,3x - 13$	75%
4	$0,1x - 8,1429$	79,03%
5	$0,0833x - 7,0833$	82,16%
6	$0,0667x - 37,333$	66,67%
7	$0,22x - 10,4$	89,63%
8	$0,2x - 21,5$	83,33%
9	$0,3x - 26,167$	96,43%
10	$0,3x - 24,667$	96,43%
11	$0,0929x - 9,9286$	88,02%
12	$0,1257x - 8,6667$	94,29%
13	$0,0255x - 3,2$	42,61%
14	$0,2x - 10$	100%
15	$0,22x - 11,5$	89,63%
16	$0,16x - 5$	94,12%
17	$0,2x - 9,5$	83,33%
18	$0,18x - 14$	60%
19	$0,4x - 22$	100%
20	$0,0667x - 10,667$	66,67%

Table 5-5 - Regression equations and determination coefficients for all participants for the Player Check task using unaltered data

The correlation values are not as good as the values for the first three tasks and the derivations are much higher. This is a common phenomenon among all the smaller tasks being measured with five second intervals. In many cases, the explanation is very simple, as even a short break of 30 seconds can lead to a very bad overall correlation if the task took the participant only about 60 to 90 seconds to complete. In the table, the correlation of participants 6 and 20 resulted from this fact. Participant 18 had a syntax error in his code, resulting in a large jump in the curve and participant 13 used a self-written method to reach the goal after achieving the first success, resulting in a longer break in editing. Interestingly enough, the Player Check task has still got a lot of good correlation values above 80%, even two values of 100%, which originate from the very few measurement points, sometimes only two. Because of the small number of test cases, the Player Check and all other smaller tasks were not well suited for data cleansing, as this often resulted in breaking down the already few entries to only one entry. Variations could have come from the time needed to search the four methods in the class.

5.2.5. The Notify Observers Task

Figure 5-8 - A sample diagram showing overall unaltered progress of participant 16 on the Notify Observers task

Nr.	All	
	Equation	R^2
1	0,145x - 11,455	96,99%
2	0,1291x - 9,5755	90,24%
3	0,2105x - 16,053	89,9%
4	0,1078x - 8,4672	92,96%
5	0,0659x - 13,509	95,22%
6	0,0425x - 10,604	86,73%
7	0,1028x - 11,045	85,42%
8	0,0243x + 0,6892	79,93%
9	0,1135x - 3,1763	88,15%
10	0,2268x - 13,195	92,89%
11	0,0758x - 4,5408	92,2%
12	0,1075x - 5,7911	95,62%
13	0,1125x - 9,2746	96,25%
14	0,1123x - 11,139	86,03%
15	0,1714x - 8,5143	84,65%
16	0,1615x - 8,3692	97,48%
17	0,2035x - 9,2045	90,01%
18	0,0748x + 0,8016	86,35%
19	0,1719x - 4,0895	92,16%
20	0,0147x - 0,9771	84,37%

Table 5-6 - Regression equations and determination coefficients for all participants for the Notify Observers task using unaltered data

The Notify Observers Task was the largest of the tasks measured in five second intervals. It therefore has a lot of good correlation values and no bolters below 70%.

The diagram and the diagrams of most other participants show that, because of the smaller time intervals, some larger dents can appear in the curve, even if correlation values are still good.

As the code needed for solving the task only had to be written once and then could be copied straight, the only variations could have arisen from the time the participants needed to search for all spots in the code where the code had to be inserted.

5.2.6. The Observers Null Task

Because it built right upon the Notify Observers Task, this task was special in editing, which can be seen in the results achieved for this task. There was a general phenomenon which showed during video analysis: Many participants did not use the copy and paste approach on this task, they rather used a find and replace approach, some even used replace all. This has lead to very few measurement points or very big leaps in the success count in a matter of seconds. The first of the two diagrams below shows a participant who took the copy and paste approach, the second shows a participant who took the find and replace approach.

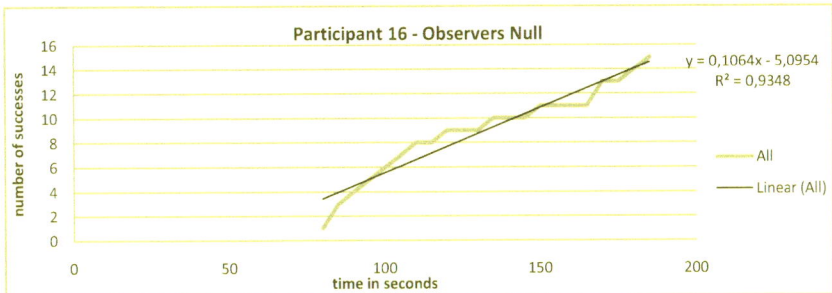

Figure 5-9 - A sample diagram showing overall unaltered progress of participant 16 on the Observers Null task, using the copy and paste approach

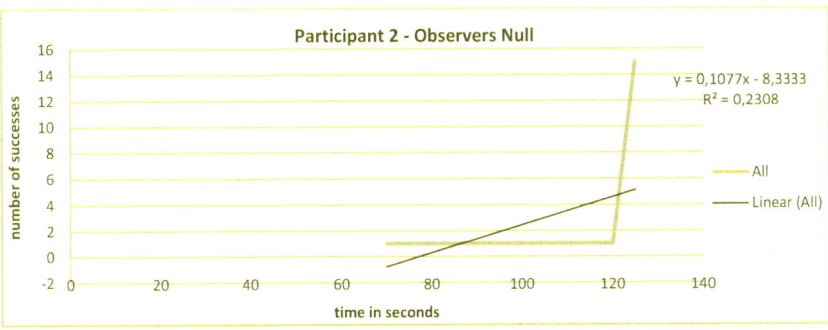

Figure 5-10 - Figure 5-11 - A sample diagram showing overall unaltered progress of participant 2 on the Observers Null task, using the find and replace approach

It can be seen very clearly that according to the progress in the second diagram, participant 2 wrote the necessary code for the first successes, and then used the find and replace approach to quickly solve the rest of the task in a matter of seconds. The video footage confirmed that this approach was taken.

Nr.	All	
	Equation	R²
1	NA	NA
2	0,1077x - 8,3333	23,08%
3	NA	NA
4	0,0789x - 11,435	92,76%
5	0,0843x - 4,6581	92,31%
6	0,0601x - 8,666	92,63%
7	NA	NA
8	0,2064x - 16,971	96,1%
9	0,1116x - 21,005	95,47%
10	NA	NA
11	0,0715x - 12,103	77,43%
12	NA	NA
13	NA	NA
14	0,0806x - 1,8703	89,38%
15	NA	NA
16	0,1064x - 5,0954	93,48%
17	0,1344x - 18,951	94,84%
18	NA	NA
19	0,1273x - 8,5455	25%
20	0,0413x - 12,474	90,66%

Table 5-7 - Regression equations and determination coefficients for all participants for the Observers Null task using unaltered data

The table clearly shows the difference between the approaches. Those who used the copy and paste approach produced overall good results in correlation, and those who used the find and replace approach produced very bad correlation or no line at all, because there was only one measurement point where all successes were fulfilled. Creating time lines does not seem to be a good instrument to measure progress using the find and replace approach. If it is to be used, it would need absolutely precise and fine-grained time intervals (possibly in the area of milliseconds) to register any small changes in successes at all. The data gathered during the experiment does not necessarily provide this precision.

5.2.7. The Refresh Constraint Task

Consisting of only eight methods to be edited, the Refresh Constraint Task was neither the smallest, nor the largest of the five second interval tasks. It still provides nice correlation results, as the diagram and table show.

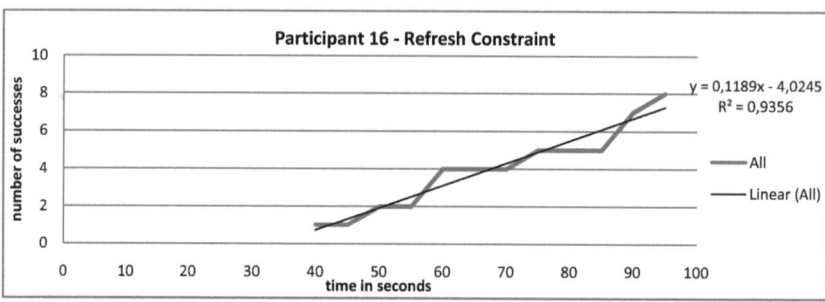

Figure 5-12 - A sample diagram showing overall unaltered progress of participant 16 on the Refresh Constraint task

Progress can now be easily spotted on the diagram, as the line nearly turns into a stairway with an overall linear appearance.

Nr.	All	
	Equation	R^2
1	0,0704x - 2,5613	88,63%
2	0,1059x - 7,7451	89,62%
3	0,0698x - 2,3354	87,47%
4	0,0779x - 6,4105	94,2%
5	0,063x - 4,3478	89,5%
6	0,0618x - 5,3062	94,86%
7	0,0765x - 4,4615	76,11%
8	0,0902x - 29,425	91,57%
9	0,009x + 0,0366	9,68%[1]
10	0,0768x - 13,009	84,27%
11	0,0645x - 3,3907	88,01%
12	0,0704x - 4,2143	89,63%
13	0,0422x - 3,6076	95,06%
14	0,0826x - 3,8273	94,77%
15	0,2167x - 15,389	89,26%
16	0,1189x - 4,0245	93,56%
17	0,1121x - 6,5714	93,83%
18	0,0892x - 4,7696	90,68%
19	0,0275x - 0,9216	16,67%[2]
20	0,0209x - 0,7354	72,72%

Table 5-8 - Regression equations and determination coefficients for all participants for the Refresh Constraint task using unaltered data

Besides two exceptions, the overall correlation values are good for this task, even with the five second interval and the few measurement points.

The values are not as good as for the larger tasks, but they are still good considering the greater derivation inserted by the small overall time and the five seconds interval.

The eight methods to be edited were pretty close together in the class, so the variation of searching the methods in the code can be neglected, leaving only the adjustment of the code for each method as a source of variation.

5.2.8. The Label Value Check Task

The Label Value Check Task displays the same progress scheme as did the Refresh Constraint task, the progress line turning into a more or less stretched or squeezed stairway for nearly every participant.

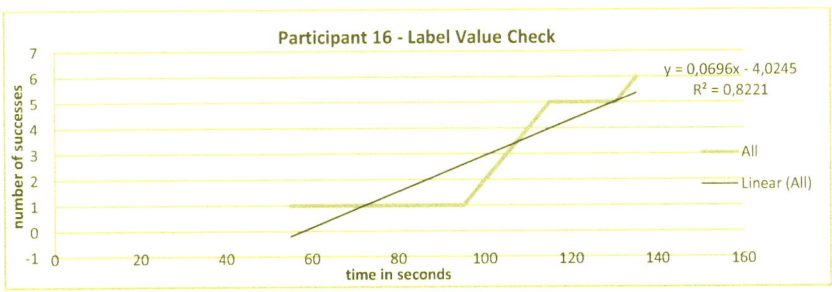

Figure 5-13 - A sample diagram showing overall unaltered progress of participant 16 on the Label Value Check task

[1] Source of bad correlation: Participant used the copy and paste approach but did the necessary adjustment after copying the raw code into every method, resulting in no compilable code the whole time.
[2] No video footage was available to explain the bad correlation. Possibly the same approach was taken as by participant 9.

Nr.	All	
	Equation	R²
1	NA	NA
2	0,0729x - 5,9071	96,76%
3	0,1091x - 7,0909	94,41%
4	0,0881x - 31,691	96,82%
5	0,0422x - 7,9788	94,74%
6	0,059x - 17,218	95,92%
7	0,1133x - 9,2333	87,58%
8	0,0299x - 7,2419	82,53%
9	0,1333x - 47,333	88,89%
10	0,0255x - 1,6242	82,4%
11	0,0347x - 6,4012	93,73%
12	0,08x - 7,0571	96,52%
13	0,0514x - 7,2426	83,72%
14	0,0514x - 7,2426	92,53%
15	0,1055x - 7,5455	95,57%
16	0,0696x - 4,0245	82,21%
17	0,0881x - 3,4953	96,82%
18	0,0585x - 4,2008	82,51%
19	0,0771x - 19,438	92,71%
20	0,036x - 8,5961	89,69%

Table 5-9 - Regression equations and determination coefficients for all participants for the Label Value Check task using unaltered data

Correlation values are good, which is surprising for such a small task. No participant falls out of the general correlation window, either. Not even one ends below 70%.

The variation of the time lines for the method searching can be neglected because the positioning of the methods was pretty similar to that of the previous task of the Refresh Constraint.

5.2.9. The Level Check Task

For this task, the results are very confusing. There is no real pattern in the way the diagrams appear or the participants solved the task. Some used the plain copy and paste approach and others used the find and replace approach. But among these approaches, variations are very strong. It turned out that some participants got caught by a small pitfall in the task description. It said that one method which fit the overall task instructions had not to be touched, because otherwise the test cases would not run correctly. Some erroneously edited that method, too and needed some time to find out about their mistake.

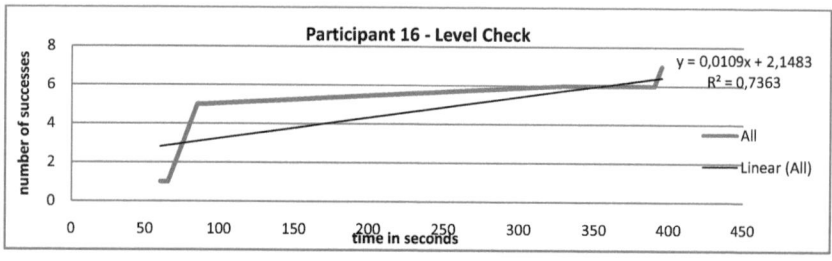

Figure 5-14 – A sample diagram showing overall unaltered progress of participant 16 on the Level Check task

Nr.	All	
	Equation	R^2
1	$0,1x - 15$	33,33%
2	0,0235x - 2,2941	16,67%
3	NA	NA
4	0,0626x - 7,5563	80%
5	0,0243x - 1,251	83,44%
6	0,0355x - 3,8767	63,84%
7	0,0646x - 5,6651	76,95%
8	0,0043x + 2,934	23,85%
9	0,051x - 5,9789	48,57%
10	NA	NA
11	0,0235x - 3,5891	66,69%
12	0,0545x - 7,7273	25%
13	0,0545x - 7,7273	16,67%
14	NA	NA
15	0,0386x + 0,0609	56,2%
16	0,0109x + 2,1483	73,63%
17	0,0538x - 3,1639	63,45%
18	NA	NA
19	0,0343x - 1,9143	20%
20	0,0596x - 12,561	89,03%

Table 5-10 - Regression equations and determination coefficients for all participants for the Level Check task using unaltered data

The diagram above shows the progress of participant 16, who used the copy and paste approach and did not make any mistakes during editing. The regression equation and correlation table shows the confusing overall results.

Those participants with no or very bad correlation used the find and replace approach, which seems similar to the results from the Observers Null task. But even those who did not necessarily use the find and replace approach seemed to make some mistakes during editing (like editing the named method and requiring some time to find out about), resulting in an overall worse correlation. All in all, the results for this task are the least clear and definite.

5.2.10. Results of the Development Times and Descriptive Statistics

To gain a better overview of the data, the results were broken down to the number of seconds the participants needed for each task. As already mentioned above, in order to measure the time required for each task using the object-oriented as well as the aspect-oriented approach, the distance was measured between the time when developers first performed any changes in the code base for a given task and the first snapshot where all test cases were fulfilled for this task.

In Table 5-11Table 5-1, all times the developers needed to complete each tasks using the aspect-oriented and the object-oriented way are shown. It can be seen that for example participant 1 required 4585 seconds to solve the logging task in the object-oriented and 4941 seconds to complete it in the aspect-oriented way.

Participant Nr.	Logging		Parameter Null		Synchronization		Player Check		Notify Observers		Observers Null		Refresh Constraint		Label Value Check		Level Check	
	AO	OO	AO	OO	AO	OO	AO	OO	AO	OO	AO	OO	AO	OO	AO	OO	AO	OO
1	4941	4585	466	1139	1138	521	334	29	631	162	429	207	185	138	1541	232	1100	70
2	876	4951	1183	712	604	452	177	42	453	151	695	91	282	104	4078	125	889	143
3	2287	3044	384	797	389	424	543	32	893	128	152	28	496	146	725	80	492	194
4	4945	7976	2751	891	877	1443	642	70	1404	201	266	236	660	160	3688	371	2340	227
5	5497	6347	480	2065	773	870	1600	109	5442	292	1003	185	574	138	2153	196	789	278
6	5046	7300	545	1094	1504	963	532	133	1271	365	1238	313	299	190	929	233	760	158
7	690	2869	300	723	223	481	195	41	244	220	181	153	162	79	465	111	238	160
8	3787	4744	384	1523	1667	382	221	102	806	466	632	149	265	367	1485	265	546	986
9	9956	4855	926	986	1344	405	526	79	3222	165	279	10	232	172	2822	299	1598	129
10	2610	2643	542	762	558	423	215	78	1413	88	881	13	253	106	3662	305	676	34
11	8175	12269	404	943	1293	634	1651	87	717	228	294	316	1074	130	2761	275	1067	298
12	7206	5014	1539	1806	1024	692	670	66	521	215	2196	198	481	137	2837	146	1195	104
13	901	3820	266	659	382	274	238	137	870	167	683	167	499	220	416	224	530	213
14	595	3383	444	777	269	477	176	49	177	195	171	183	400	122	910	236	282	205
15	3799	2755	377	448	851	301	197	32	2250	97	119	131	322	62	333	97	621	189
16	2033	3030	148	470	248	502	383	22	189	127	273	178	310	85	734	120	241	382
17	711	3278	218	641	224	392	165	44	483	131	310	170	403	85	459	100	250	165
18	4544	4615	445	713	554	510	320	86	2051	231	551	174	818	113	1729	162	2622	436
19	3598	3060	237	460	302	451	259	53	1627	107	774	82	276	105	934	294	872	86
20	5103	6733	5193	1098	1184	961	503	80	750	731	298	376	344	278	4359	200	899	179

Table 5-11 – Development times for every participant and every task, measured in seconds

Next, the values of the aspect-oriented times were then subtracted from the object-oriented values, to gain an understanding when each participant was faster using aspect-orientation and how much faster he or she was.

Negative values mean that the participant was faster using aspect-orientation. There still seems to be no clear or significant pattern among the participants' progress. An interesting phenomenon is that the cases in which participants were faster using the aspect-oriented way for the smaller tasks (Player Check to Level Check) are very rare, and if they appear, the time difference seems quite marginal. This hardens the thesis that (when looking at the time facet of development only) aspect-orientation makes sense if it helps to avoid writing a certain amount of redundant code, but from which amount the advantage of aspect-orientation starts is still not sure. These results seem as they might have been expectable for the small tasks and that was exactly what the small tasks were designed for.

Participant	Logging Δ	Param. Null Δ	Sync. Δ	Player C. Δ	Notify O. Δ	Obs. Null Δ	Refresh C. Δ	Label V.C. Δ	Level C. Δ
1	356	-673	617	305	469	222	47	1309	1030
2	-4075	471	152	135	302	604	178	3953	746
3	-757	-413	-35	511	765	124	350	645	298
4	-3031	1860	-566	572	1203	30	500	3317	2113
5	-850	-1585	-97	1491	5150	818	436	1957	511
6	-2254	-549	541	399	906	925	109	696	602
7	-2179	-423	-258	154	24	28	83	354	78
8	-957	-1139	1285	119	340	483	-102	1220	-440
9	5101	-60	939	447	3057	269	60	2523	1469
10	-33	-220	135	137	1325	868	147	3357	642
11	-4094	-539	659	1564	489	-22	944	2486	769
12	2192	-267	332	604	306	1998	344	2691	1091
13	-2919	-393	108	101	703	516	279	192	317
14	-2788	-333	-208	127	-18	-12	278	674	77
15	1044	-71	550	165	2153	-12	260	236	432
16	-997	-322	-254	361	62	95	225	614	-141
17	-2567	-423	-168	121	352	140	318	359	85
18	-71	-268	44	234	1820	377	705	1567	2186
19	538	-223	-149	206	1520	692	171	640	786
20	-1630	4095	223	423	19	-78	66	4159	720

Table 5-12 – Differences between aspect-oriented and object-oriented development times

Because the mass of information of the raw data does not seem to be very meaningful, some descriptive statistics functions were performed on the data to get a better impression of the overall meaning the data presents. Functions used are (in the same order are as listed in the table from top to bottom) the sum, maximum, minimum, arithmetical average, median and standard derivation (arithmetical average, median and standard derivation were also calculated for the deltas). In addition, the total ratio of aspect-oriented to object-oriented time and the number of values where aspect-orientation helped solve the task faster were calculated. All these were performed only on the raw data and on the deltas from Table 5-12.

Function	Logging		Parameter Null		Synchronization		Player Check		Notify Observers		Observers Null		Refresh Constraint		Label Value Check		Level Check	
	AO	OO	AO	OO	AO	OO	AO	OO	AO	OO	AO	OO	AO	OO	AO	OO	AO	OO
Σ	77300	97271	17232	18707	15408	11558	9547	1371	25414	4467	11425	3360	8335	2937	37020	4071	18007	4636
max	9956	12269	5193	2065	1667	1443	1651	137	5442	731	2196	376	1074	367	4359	371	2622	986
min	595	2643	148	448	223	274	165	22	177	88	119	10	162	62	333	80	238	34
∅	3865	4864	862	935	770	578	477	69	1271	223	571	168	417	147	1851	204	900	232
med	3793	4600	445	787	689	479	327	68	838	181	370	172	333	134	1513	212	775	184
σ	2627	2356	1184	432	464	284	426	34	1251	151	494	97	226	73	1344	83	647	203
∅ Δ	-999		-74		193		409		1047		403		270		1647		669	
med Δ	-977		-328		122		270		596		246		243		1265		622	
σ Δ	2218,61		1177,50		457,26		415,58		1260,30		496,17		241,54		1311,41		674,41	
Σ$_{ao}$/Σ$_{oo}$	79,47%		92,12%		133,31%		696,35%		568,93%		340,03%		283,79%		909,36%		388,42%	
#(Δ<0)	15		17		8		0		1		4		1		0		2	

Table 5-13 – Descriptive statistics for the development times of all participants

When looking at the ratios and comparing them to each other, only the first two tasks seem to be solved faster by most participants using aspect-orientation (later, some statistical tests are used to try to harden the evidence) and the rest of the tasks suffers from very big differences in overall time in favor of the object-oriented approach. Again, these results were almost certainly predictable for the smaller tasks. Only the Synchronization task falls out of the picture, because it was a larger task where the aspect for its solving was not very complicated, but the overall ratio still speaks in favor of the object-oriented approach.

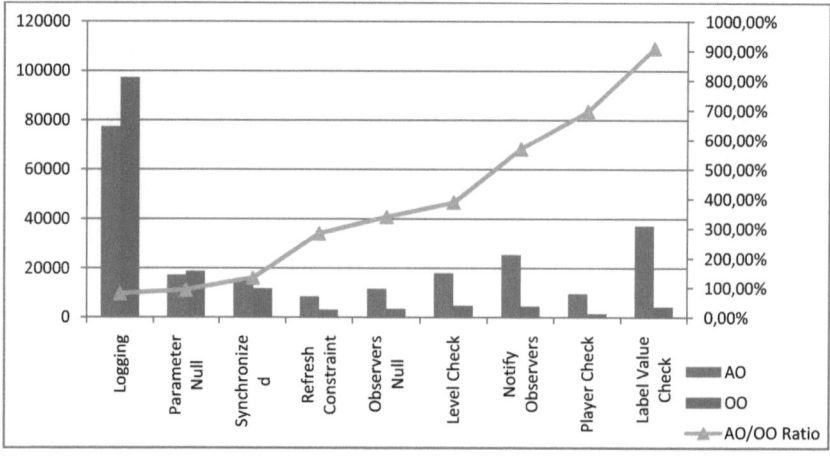

Figure 5-15 - Sum of times for the object-oriented and aspect-oriented solutions and the ratio $\sum ao / \sum oo$

Figure 5-15 graphically describes the sums of times requires for the object-oriented and aspect-oriented task. The axis on the left hand side describes the time in seconds (where the bars represent the time sum for the tasks from the table above) and the axis on the right hand side describes the percentage (where the lines in the figure with the corresponding dots represent the aspect-oriented to object-oriented ratio for each task). The line was drawn for better clarity, not for semantics. The tasks on the x-axis are ordered ascending by their ratios to show the increasing values, especially for the smaller tasks.

Although the aggregated values already give some overview of the possible impact of using an aspect-orientation approach for solving the corresponding task, it is necessary to have a closer look on each participant. This is due to two reasons: First, the aggregated values do not consider that developers largely vary in their development speed. Hence, if ratios for each participant are compared, it removes the individual development speed of each participant on the resulting statistics. Second, because of the high standard derivations of all tasks it is necessary to have a close look to each participant's data in order to determine whether there is also a large variety among the ratios for each participant. So, until now, the data was evaluated and compared on an inter-participant base.

The next tables and statistics will focus on an intra-participant evaluation. First, all ratios of aspect-orientation to object-orientation are listed for each task and participant. Another table shows some statistics on these values. All values are shown as percentages, where a ratio of 100% means aspect-orientation took as long as the object-oriented approach, ratios lesser than 100% mean aspect-orientation was faster and vice-versa.

Table 5-14 describes the ratios for each participant, i.e. the ratios where the absolute times are removed. The impression with respect to the time for each task is slightly more chaotic. If concentrating only on the comparison of the logging task and the parameter null task, it can be seen that seven participants have a higher ratio for the first task than the second task, even if the aspect for the second task was supposedly easier to write. There are even dramatic differences among these ratios. For example, the differences of the ratios for participant 20 are more than 400% (where the logging task has a relatively good ratio) while for participant nine the difference is more than 1000% (whereby the logging task has a larger ratio). Furthermore, there are even participants whose ratio in one task dramatically differs from the other participants and tasks. For example, participant 20 displays an extraordinary high ratio for the Parameter Null task, while having had quite a good ratio for the Logging task and some of the smaller ones.

Participant Nr.	Logging	Parameter Null	Synchronization	Player Check	Notify Observers	Observers Null	Refresh Constraint	Label Value Check	Level Check
					Task				
	t_{ao}/t_{oo}	t_{ao}/t_{oo}	t_{ao}/t_{oo}	t_{ao}/t_{oo}	t_{ao}/t_{oo}	t_{ao}/t_{oo}	t_{ao}/t_{oo}	t_{ao}/t_{oo}	t_{ao}/t_{oo}
1	107,76%	40,91%	218,43%	1151,72%	389,51%	207,25%	134,06%	664,22%	1571,43%
2	17,69%	166,15%	133,63%	421,43%	300,00%	763,74%	271,15%	3262,40%	621,68%
3	75,13%	48,18%	91,75%	1696,88%	697,66%	542,86%	339,73%	906,25%	253,61%
4	62,00%	308,75%	60,78%	917,14%	698,51%	112,71%	412,50%	994,07%	1030,84%
5	86,61%	23,24%	88,85%	1467,89%	1863,70%	542,16%	415,94%	1098,47%	283,81%
6	69,12%	49,82%	156,18%	400,00%	348,22%	395,53%	157,37%	398,71%	481,01%
7	24,05%	41,49%	46,36%	475,61%	110,91%	118,30%	205,06%	418,92%	148,75%
8	79,83%	25,21%	436,39%	216,67%	172,96%	424,16%	72,21%	560,38%	55,38%
9	205,07%	93,91%	331,85%	665,82%	1952,73%	2790,00%	134,88%	943,81%	1238,76%
10	98,75%	71,13%	131,91%	275,64%	1605,68%	6776,92%	238,68%	1200,66%	1988,24%
11	66,63%	42,84%	203,94%	1897,70%	314,47%	93,04%	826,15%	1004,00%	358,05%
12	143,72%	85,22%	147,98%	1015,15%	242,33%	1109,09%	351,09%	1943,15%	1149,04%
13	23,59%	40,36%	139,42%	173,72%	520,96%	408,98%	226,82%	185,71%	248,83%
14	17,59%	57,14%	56,39%	359,18%	90,77%	93,44%	327,87%	385,59%	137,56%
15	137,89%	84,15%	282,72%	615,63%	2319,59%	90,84%	519,35%	343,30%	328,57%
16	67,10%	31,49%	49,40%	1740,91%	148,82%	153,37%	364,71%	611,67%	63,09%
17	21,69%	34,01%	57,14%	375,00%	368,70%	182,35%	474,12%	459,00%	151,52%
18	98,46%	62,41%	108,63%	372,09%	887,88%	316,67%	723,89%	1067,28%	601,38%
19	117,58%	51,52%	66,96%	488,68%	1520,56%	943,90%	262,86%	317,69%	1013,95%
20	75,79%	472,95%	123,20%	628,75%	102,60%	79,26%	123,74%	2179,50%	502,23%

Table 5-14 – Ratios of aspect-oriented to object-oriented development time

It seems very hard to tell whether a participant would have a good ratio on all tasks when looking at one task ratio. So, predicting the other results from one or two ratios would not work for most participants. A meanwhile well-known fact seems to manifest again in the ratios, as values below 100% get extremely rare for the smaller tasks. To aggregate the data into a better understandable overview, the following functions were applied to it: The sum, maximum, minimum, arithmetical average, median and standard derivation.

Function	Task								
	Logging	Parameter Null	Synchronization	Player Check	Notify Observers	Observers Null	Refresh Constraint	Label Value Check	Level Check
Σ	1596,05%	1830,91%	2931,92%	15355,62%	14656,54%	16144,57%	6582,19%	18944,79%	12227,72%
max	205,07%	472,95%	436,39%	1897,70%	2319,59%	6776,92%	826,15%	3262,40%	1988,24%
min	17,59%	23,24%	46,36%	173,72%	90,77%	79,26%	72,21%	185,71%	55,38%
∅	79,80%	91,55%	146,60%	767,78%	732,83%	807,23%	329,11%	947,24%	611,39%
med	75,46%	50,67%	127,56%	552,15%	379,10%	356,10%	299,51%	785,24%	419,53%
σ	48,28%	110,51%	103,49%	545,60%	710,47%	1534,41%	196,24%	753,80%	544,73%

Table 5-15 – Statistical functions on the ratio data

The differences between minimum and maximum for the smaller tasks are much higher than for the first three larger tasks. Furthermore, especially for the observer task a much higher standard derivation compared to the other tasks can be seen, while the standard derivations for the parameter null task and synchronization tasks are almost equal. Only the first two tasks display an average or median that is below 100% and task three has a value just above 100%, but for all other tasks the average and median values jump extremely high.

After evaluating the development times in absolute and relative ways, no clear picture concerning the results has appeared so far. The only thing that seems to be very sure is the disadvantageous performance of aspect-orientation for small tasks. The logging and parameter null tasks seem to be the two tasks where most participants (independently from their absolute development times) achieve better results using aspect-orientation. There is also a very huge gap between the development times of the participants, which can be seen best from the absolute development time minimum and maximum values. Finally, there are noteworthy differences in the relative development times where it looks like that for certain developers the application of aspect-oriented techniques can have a positive impact as well as a dramatic negative impact on the development speed. Hence, even if there is large number of redundant code lines to be specified (as for example for the logging task) the ratio for a participant might be even higher than in cases where less redundant code lines have to be specified, creating an overall confusing picture. However, the descriptive data reveals some tendencies for the comparison of aspect-oriented techniques and object-oriented techniques for specifying redundant code. Nevertheless, in order to check whether any of those tendencies are significant, corresponding tests have to be performed which will be done in the next section.

5.2.11. Statistical Tests on the Results

In preparation of the statistical tests, a visualization attempt using scatter diagrams was made and paints a better picture for the distribution of the values. The diagrams were split, showing the first three larger tasks for aspect-orientation and object-orientation each, and the same for the smaller tasks. The diagrams were split because the larger and smaller tasks cannot be compared well on an absolute time foundation.

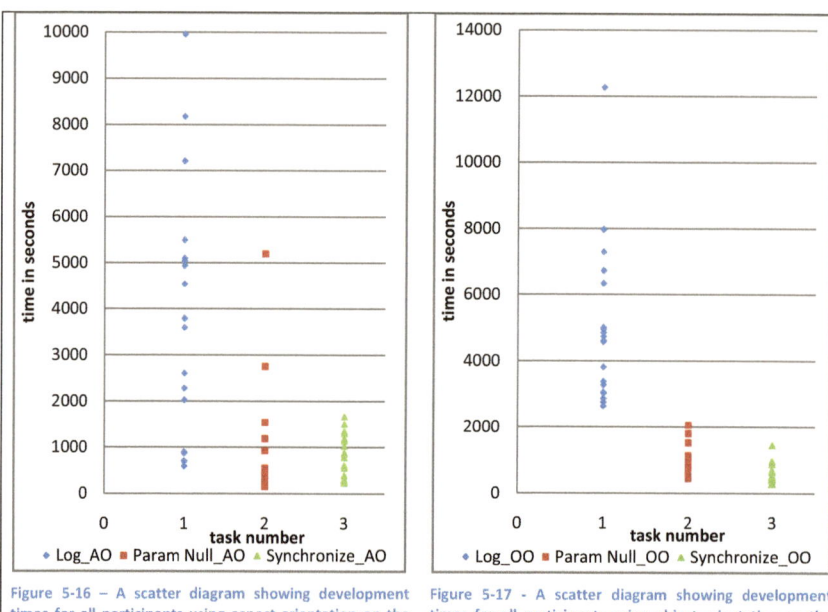

Figure 5-16 – A scatter diagram showing development times for all participants using aspect-orientation on the larger three tasks

Figure 5-17 - A scatter diagram showing development times for all participants using object-orientation on the larger three tasks

It can be seen that the variance among the points of the left diagram is greater than the variance of the points from the right diagram. The object-oriented results seem to be grouped tighter together, have less mavericks and the standard derivation is generally higher among all tasks for the aspect-oriented results (some descriptive values are shown in a later table).

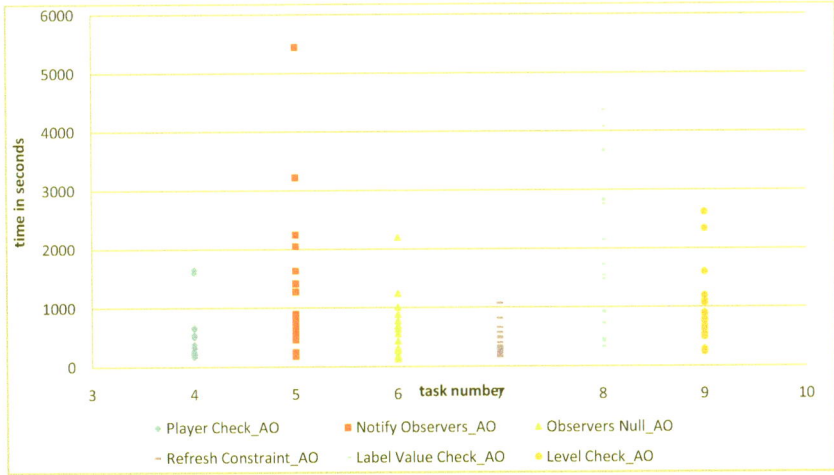

Figure 5-18 - A scatter diagram showing development times for all participants using aspect-orientation on the smaller six tasks.

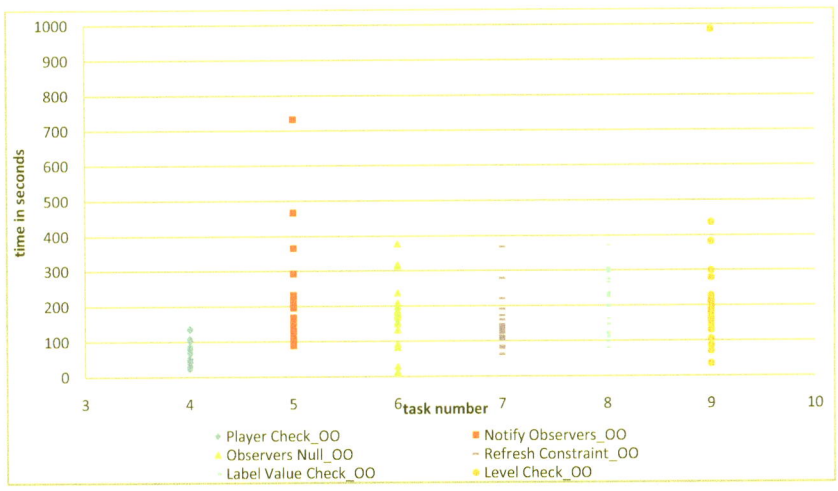

Figure 5-19 - A scatter diagram showing development times for all participants using object-orientation on the smaller six tasks.

The impression of the first two diagrams returns for Figure 5-18 and Figure 5-19, although it seems from the diagrams that the relative differences among the tasks are not as big for each approach as they are for the larger tasks, but this impression may result from the overall smaller time intervals.

To test whether any of these results are significant, statistical tests will have to be used on the data. The standard test for finding significance in data is the t-test, whose premise is that the used data is normally distributed. So the first task was to check whether the resulting data (in this case, the absolute development times that were discussed thoroughly in the last sub-chapter) actually fulfills this premise. Two statistical tests were performed for this check: The Kolmogorov-Smirnov-test and the Shapiro-Wilk-test.[1] The results can be found below. The Hypothesis for the Kolmogorov-Smirnov-test and Shapiro-Wilk-test is that the data the test is performed on has its source in a normally distributed set. If the significance of each test is below 5%, the hypothesis can be rejected for this particular set of data.

- H0: The development time results of an approach for a specific task originates from a normally distributed population

- H1: The results do not originate from a normally distributed population

Task	Kolmogorov-Smirnov			Shapiro-Wilk		
	Statistics	df	Significance	Statistics	df	Significance
Logging AO	0,120	20	0,200	0,931	20	0,161
Logging OO	0,225	20	0,009	0,816	20	0,001
Param Null AO	0,355	20	0,000	0,565	20	0,000
Param Null OO	0,176	20	0,107	0,861	20	0,008
Synchronization AO	0,144	20	0,200	0,921	20	0,103
Synchronization OO	0,279	20	0,000	0,801	20	0,001
Player Check AO	0,239	20	0,004	0,686	20	0,000
Player Check OO	0,127	20	0,200	0,940	20	0,237
Notify Observers AO	0,219	20	0,013	0,759	20	0,000
Notify Observers OO	0,280	20	0,000	0,741	20	0,000
Observers Null AO	0,201	20	0,033	0,787	20	0,001
Observers Null OO	0,143	20	0,200	0,948	20	0,338
Refresh Constraint AO	0,176	20	0,105	0,854	20	0,006
Refresh Constraint OO	0,205	20	0,028	0,836	20	0,003
Label Value Check AO	0,203	20	0,031	0,888	20	0,025
Label Value Check OO	0,127	20	0,200	0,954	20	0,427
Level Check AO	0,201	20	0,034	0,835	20	0,003
Level Check OO	0,259	20	0,001	0,682	20	0,000

Table 5-16 – Results of the statistical tests for normal distribution

From the results in Table 5-16, it can be seen that most of the result sets do not get a significance value of above 5%. Even if some do get a slightly better significance to reach the used significance level (like the Logging aspect-orientation times for both tests), the overall picture does not provide strong enough evidence, as no pair of values for a task presents a good significance value for both. This means the H0 hypothesis does not hold for any pair of times. Hence, the two test results

---

[1] Mathematical Background can inter alia be found at
http://en.wikipedia.org/wiki/Kolmogorov%E2%80%93Smirnov_test and
http://en.wikipedia.org/wiki/Shapiro%E2%80%93Wilk_test (the Kolkmogorov-Smirnov test uses a significance correction by Lilliefors)

contradict the assumption of a normal distribution and therefore this hypothesis should be rejected, making the sets unusable for use with a t-test. It cannot be said why the tests result in such bad significance values, maybe the data from the 20 participants is not enough to give stronger results or the values of the development times are much too scattered for any cohesion.

Still, a Wilcoxon-test[1] can be performed on the data pairs, which compares the medians of two sets with the hypothesis that both are equal. The significance value represents the probability that the examinations resulted from random effects and a low value therefore means a possible stronger trend that both sets are really different, which is a good result.

H0: The medians of the aspect-oriented and object-oriented times for a task are equal.

H1: The medians for the times are not equal.

Task		N	avg. Rank	rank sum	Z	asymptotic significance
Logging	neg. ranks	5	9,60	48,00	-2,128	0,033
	pos. Ranks	15	10,80	162,00		
Parameter Null	neg. ranks	3	17,33	52,00	-1,979	0,048
	pos. Ranks	17	9,29	158,00		
Synchronization	neg. ranks	12	12,00	144,00	-1,456	0,145
	pos. Ranks	8	8,25	66,00		
Player Check	neg. ranks	20	10,50	210,00	-3,92	0,000
	pos. Ranks	0	,00	,00		
Notify Observers	neg. ranks	19	11,00	209,00	-3,883	0,000
	pos. Ranks	1	1,00	1,00		
Observers Null	neg. ranks	16	12,38	198,00	-3,472	0,001
	pos. Ranks	4	3,00	12,00		
Refresh Constraint	neg. ranks	19	10,79	205,00	-3,733	0,000
	pos. Ranks	1	5,00	5,00		
Label Value Check	neg. ranks	20	10,50	210,00	-3,92	0,000
	pos. Ranks	0	,00	,00		
Level Check	neg. ranks	18	11,00	198,00	-3,472	0,001
	pos. Ranks	2	6,00	12,00		

Table 5-17 – Results of the Wilcoxon-test

In this case, negative ranks are data entries where aspect-orientation took a longer time to complete than object-orientation. There seems to be a strong difference between both approaches, as eight of the nine results are significant for a significance level of 0.05, which is a good sign because it tells us that the results of both approaches are significantly different from each other and the H0 hypothesis can be rejected for them. Eight of nine is a definite tendency towards saying that there is a definite difference in the time results for both techniques.

---

[1] Information on the Wilcoxon-test can be found here: http://en.wikipedia.org/wiki/Wilcoxon_signed-rank_test

Now, a next step is to inspect the value which derives from these results: The H0 hypothesis only holds for the Synchronization task. This is an interesting fact, as the Synchronization task also displays the most balanced values for positive and negative ranks. When looking back at the tables from the previous chapters, the Synchronized task has many of the least differences between the statistical values like maximum, minimum, average, median (which is used in the hypothesis) and its median and its average differences of the absolute times are one of the smallest (see Table 5-13). These values might be an explanation why the H0 hypothesis holds for the Synchronization task, as the values of the different participants do not seem to strongly lean forward in overall favor of any of the two approaches, even if the data from the previous analysis points toward a victory of object-orientation.

From the values of the rank sums, it can now be interpreted for each task in which case the difference tends to go, either in favor of aspect-orientation or object-orientation. Only the first two tasks seem to end in positive results for aspect-orientation. The rank numbers are similar to the numbers from Table 5-13 and the rank sums behave similarly, where the results for the smaller tasks were clearly in favor of object-oriented programming.

5.2.12. Doing a Break-Even Analysis

Because one of the primary goals of the experiment was to compare object-oriented development performance and aspect-oriented development performance on the same task, a break-even analysis of the data was done. During the analysis, the result of the aspect-oriented development time for a task was to be inserted into the regression equation from the object-oriented performance diagrams from the first analysis chapter, to get the break-even point, meaning the point where the aspect-oriented approach would have taken the corresponding developer the same time as using the object-oriented approach. If this point lies above the overall number of methods the participants had to edit for a task, the aspect-oriented approach had a negative effect on the development time for this specific participant. If it lies below, the participant was faster using aspect-orientation. To achieve more precise results, the diagram data had to be adjusted so that it was based on the same calculation as the aspect-oriented development time, meaning that the interval after starting the workspace where the developer did not touch the code had to be subtracted. This leads to a shifted normalized diagram look, not altering the slope of the regressions equation but the intercept value. The diagram below holds the same data as Figure 5-2 from the sub-chapter for task one above, where the progress for participant 16 was shown, it is just corrected by a small time interval shifting it to the left. This can be seen from the changed intercept value.

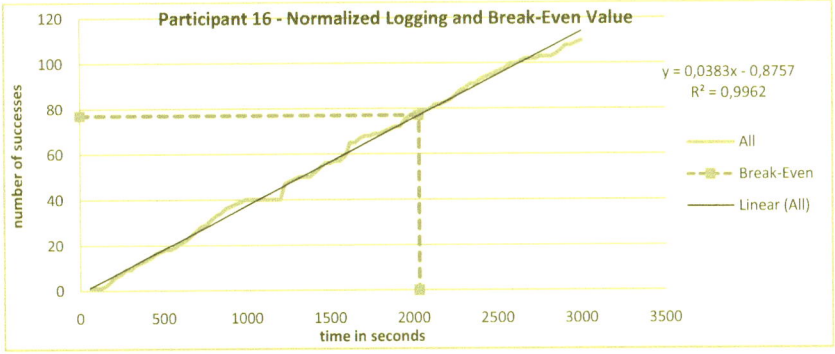

Figure 5-20 – Normalized diagram for participant 16 and the logging task

The break-even point is also shown in the diagram for this participant, which is below the maximum number of methods that had to edited for the logging task (which is 110), so this participant has had a positive impact on his development speed through aspect-orientation.

In Table 5-18, the absolute break-even values are listed for each participant, along with the descriptive statistics values in the next table. The functions performed for the raw break-even values are (in this order from top to bottom): Sum, maximum, minimum, arithmetical average, median, standard derivation. In addition, the number of total test cases (meaning number of methods that had to be edited), the number of positive break-even values compared to the total test case value and the ratio of positive break-even values (for all participants that had a measurable result) were added for additional information.

This break-even analysis again strengthens the assumption of a noticeable positive impact of aspect-orientation for tasks of a specific size. The total positive values for the first three tasks are 70% and 50%, which seems to be at least a noticeable result, but for the smaller tasks, no ratio exceeds 15% at all. There is also a very large interval between the minimum and maximum values, showing how strong the impact can vary for different developers. Interestingly enough, the number of positive break-even values does not always equal the number of positive differences from table Table 5-13. The only time where these values are the same is for the Player Check, Label Value Check and Level Check tasks. This is interesting because a positive value among the absolute time differences should also mean a positive break-even point. The only explanations for this phenomenon might be the overall rounding errors that have been introduced either into the absolute time calculation and the break-even calculation (where this even multiplies, as the diagram values have been rounded and estimated themselves and were then used in the break-even calculation using additional rounded values) resulting in inaccurate numbers. For some of the smaller tasks, the missing break-even data is surely the source of these incorrect values.

Participant Number	Logging	Parameter Null	Synchronization	Player Check	Notify Observers	Observers Null	Refresh Constraint	Label Value Check	Level Check
1	127	20	136	54	91	-	13	-	109
2	15	61	57	32	75	73	27	295	20
3	90	20	43	158	139	-	35	76	-
4	53	103	26	61	154	17	49	300	143
5	94	14	47	130	358	85	34	89	20
6	83	25	62	31	57	72	16	47	26
7	7	21	22	43	22	-	13	48	13
8	83	20	221	32	133	120	-1[1]	44	6
9	260	24	122	144	368	22	2	345	80
10	115	25	63	52	321	-	19	92	-
11	77	15	117	149	50	14	69	92	24
12	172	35	71	82	56	-	33	223	63
13	7	51	33	6	100	-	20	17	10
14	14	21	30	33	10	16	32	25	-
15	159	278	104	44	386	-	67	33	26
16	77	12	27	62	30	27	37	49	5
17	14	13	34	33	99	36	46	39	14
18	98	22	50	50	335	-	71	100	-
19	126	17	25	97	282	95	8	55	30
20	83	180	66	32	13	25	9	155	50

Table 5-18 – Break-even values for all participants and all tasks

Function	Logging	Parameter Null	Synchronization	Player Check	Notify Observers	Observers Null	Refresh Constraint	Label Value Check	Level Check
Σ	1754	976	1356	1327	3078	603	601	2125	640
max	260	278	221	158	386	120	71	345	143
min	7	12	22	6	10	14	-1	17	5
∅	88	49	68	66	154	50	30	112	40
med	83	22	54	51	100	32	29	76	25
σ	63	67	50	45	133	37	22	102	40
# tc	110	34	52	4	19	15	8	6	7
# pos.	14	14	10	0	2	1	3	0	2
% pos.	70,00%	70,00%	50,00%	0,00%	10,00%	8,33%	15,00%	0,00%	12,50%

Table 5-19 – Descriptive Statistics on the break-even values

[1] The negative value results from a calculation where the regression line intersects the aspect-oriented development time point below the x-axis. This can happen due to long object-oriented time with a sharp slope at the end of the curve and a very short aspect-oriented time.

The total trend can be read from the next diagram, where the distribution of the break-even values (shown as absolute times on the y-axis) is shown along with the corresponding threshold value (the maximum number of test cases for that task) for each task numbered from one to nine (x-axis). The amount of points above the threshold line is very large for the small tasks.

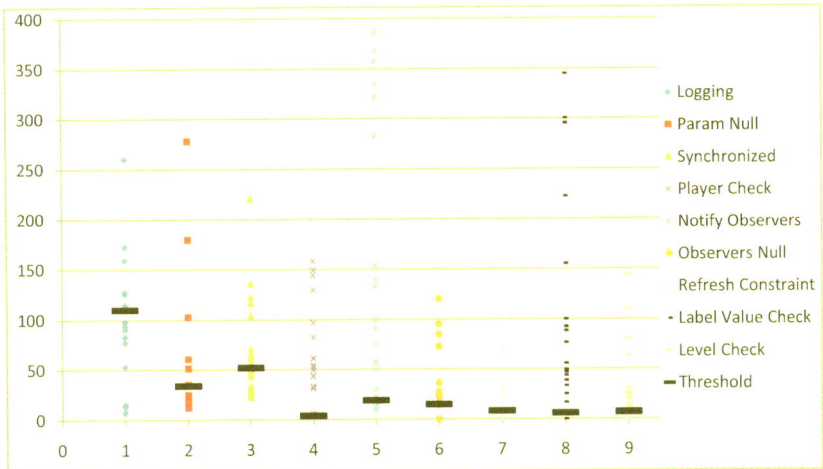

Figure 5-21 – Scatter diagram for the distribution of the break-even values for all tasks

All values are of course relative, because the overall time difference between the developers is not considered here. A developer who needed 1500 seconds for an aspect-oriented solution and 3000 for the object-oriented can have a similar break-even ratio as a developer with the values 300 and 600. Additionally, some regression equations are very imprecise, because they consist only of two or a little more measurement points. This is the reason why the minimum values for the small tasks are pretty low, even if they should not be, considering the real performance of the developers. The real performance would be even worse than what can be seen here.

Ultimately, nothing points towards a general positive impact of aspect-orientation for the small tasks, even if looking at those participants who achieved good results for the larger tasks. Aspect-orientation does not seem to be a good choice for time savings on tasks with less than about 30 methods to be edited (the value was estimated from the number of methods for the parameter null task, which is 34, but the results of course also depend on the aspect complexity). The largest of the smaller tasks (Notify Observers) had 19 methods to be edited and still achieved bad results. A developer using a copy and paste or find and replace approach still seems to be much faster in almost every case of such small assignments.

5.2.13. Participant Grouping

Because the preceding evaluations did not yield any real significant results, a last attempt to achieve a possible generalizable statement was done using the data from the statistics and from the questionnaire taken at the beginning of the experiment. For example, participants were grouped according to their answers about overall programming and aspect-oriented experience and other factors or their performance ratios. It was then tried to find possible similarities among the top-performers. The idea behind this approach was that programmers with overall good programming skills and/or AspectJ experience should have performed best in the experiment, either through their familiarity with AspectJ or their general programming experience which helped them adjust to the mechanics of aspect-oriented programming faster than novices (or they might have even been good developers in general and were also familiar with AspectJ, being the best combination).

The grouping tries to concentrate on the ratios the participants achieved in the first three tasks, as those where the ones where the comparison of aspect-orientation and object-orientation had achieved at least some significant results. The smaller tasks' results were all equally bad, which is why they are not appropriate for a useful grouping. The five answers from the questionnaire which are directly related to the overall programming skill are summarized in Table 5-20, coded from one (worst) to six (best) on an ordinal scale. The participants were asked for an estimation of their overall development skills, their java and eclipse experience and their experience with reflection tasks and AspectJ.

Participant Nr.	1	2	3	4	5	6	7	8	9	10	11	12	13	14	15	16	17	18	19	20
Dev. Skill	5	5	6	4	5	4	5	5	5	5	4	3	4	5	5	4	6	5	6	4
Java Skill	5	5	6	4	5	4	5	4	4	5	3	3	4	4	5	3	6	5	5	4
Eclipse Skill	5	5	6	3	5	3	5	4	4	5	2	2	3	4	5	2	6	4	4	4
Reflection Skill	2	4	1	2	3	2	4	3	3	1	1	1	4	6	5	4	6	1	3	3
AspectJ Skill	1	1	1	1	1	1	5	3	3	1	1	1	2	5	3	3	2	2	1	4

Table 5-20 – Answers to the questionnaire

The data from the questionnaire was used to try and find a possible connection between the answers to certain (or all) questions and the overall performance for the first three tasks (in form of the ratios of the absolute times). With a direct comparison of the questionnaire results and the ratios it proved to be very difficult to find correlations between the questionnaire answer values and the ratios, so this approach was discarded and as an alternative the following approach was taken: First, all cases were identified where a participant had a better (smaller) ratio than the average ratio for all participants for this task. Then, the participants were grouped according to the number of larger tasks where their results were lesser than the average, resulting in the categorization of novice, average, advanced:

- **Advanced**: All participants whose ratios in these three tasks were less than the average ratios

- **Average**: All participants where the ratios in two of the tasks were less than the average ratios

- **Novices**: All participants that have less than two ratios which were less than the average.

When grouping the participants using these criteria, participants number 3, 7, 13, 14, 16 and 17 are declared as advanced programmers, participants 2, 4, 5, 6, 10, 11, 18, 19, 20 as average programmers and 9, 1, 8, 12, 15 as novices.

But this categorization seems to be only consistent for the group of the advanced programmers, who also seem to perform the best on the smaller tasks, when looking at the averages, as shown in the summary Table 5-21.

Advanced Developers					Average Developers					Novice Developers				
Participant Nr.	Logging ratio	Parameter Null ratio	Synchronization ratio	# of pos. smaller tasks	Participant Nr.	Logging ratio	Parameter Null ratio	Synchronization ratio	# of pos. smaller tasks	Participant Nr.	Logging ratio	Parameter Null ratio	Synchronization ratio	# of pos. smaller tasks
3	75,13%	48,18%	91,75%	4	2	17,69%	166,15%	133,63%	4	9	205,07%	93,91%	331,85%	3
7	24,05%	41,49%	46,36%	6	4	62,00%	308,75%	60,78%	2	1	107,76%	40,91%	218,43%	4
13	23,59%	40,36%	139,42%	6	5	86,61%	23,24%	88,85%	2	8	79,83%	25,21%	436,39%	6
14	17,59%	57,14%	56,39%	6	6	69,12%	49,82%	88,85%	6	12	143,72%	85,22%	147,98%	1
16	67,10%	31,49%	49,40%	4	10	98,75%	71,13%	131,91%	2	15	137,89%	84,15%	282,72%	4
17	21,69%	34,01%	57,14%	5	11	66,63%	42,84%	203,94%	3					
					18	98,46%	62,41%	108,63%	3					
					19	117,58%	51,52%	66,96%	3					
					20	75,79%	472,95%	123,20%	5					

Table 5-21 – Three tables showing the developer categorizations

All ratios for the first three tasks are included in the table, even those with a value greater than the average for that task. It can be seen that the advanced group really sticks out for the fulfillment of all larger tasks below average, even if not all of them are among the best when considering the pure ratios. The average and novice developer group are not as far away from each other and there appears to be another interesting fact of inconsistency shown in the descriptive statistics.

Task	Group								
	Advanced			Average			Novices		
	Logging	Parameter Null	Synchronization	Logging	Parameter Null	Synchronization	Logging	Parameter Null	Synchronization
Σ	229,14%	252,68%	440,46%	692,64%	1248,82%	1006,76%	674,27%	329,41%	1417,37%
max	75,13%	57,14%	139,42%	117,58%	472,95%	203,94%	205,07%	93,91%	436,39%
min	17,59%	31,49%	46,36%	17,69%	23,24%	60,78%	79,83%	25,21%	147,98%
∅	38,19%	42,11%	73,41%	76,96%	138,76%	111,86%	134,85%	65,88%	283,47%
med	23,82%	40,93%	56,77%	75,79%	62,41%	108,63%	137,89%	84,15%	282,72%
σ	25,73%	9,43%	36,21%	28,69%	154,03%	43,56%	46,85%	30,70%	109,90%
∅ pos.	5,17			3,33			3,6		
med pos.	5,5			3			4		

Table 5-22 – Descriptive statistics values for the participant groupings

The functions are the sum, maximum, minimum, arithmetical average, median and standard derivation. Two additional values are the average and median of the number of small tasks where the participants had a positive result (a value smaller than the average). The results for the advanced group are pretty good when compared to the other two, especially the averages and medians are significantly better. An interesting phenomenon shows in the minimum and maximum values. Some of them are better for the average and novice group than for the advanced group, indicating that some of the developers from these groups excelled at specific tasks even if their overall performance seemed not to be the best. Another inconsistency shows in the values for the averages and medians of the number of positive smaller task results. The novice group actually seems to perform better in terms of average and median values than the average group. It seems that this grouping approach does not do justice to the results of some developers, who might have accidently slipped in the wrong groups for novice and average developers. The only group whose results are mostly good is the advanced developer group.

To test whether the results of the groupings are normally distributed and the grouping results possible significant, the same statistical tests as on the raw development data was used. At first the Kolmogorov-Smirnov-test and then the Shapiro-Wilk-test were done, both performed on the absolute development times but as the grouped sets.

Tests for the advanced group

The hypotheses are equal to those from the tests above, except for the fact that they only concentrate on the grouped sets of data.

- H0: The development time results for a group originate from a normally distributed population
- H1: The results do not originate from a normally distributed population

First, the normal distribution tests are shown for the advanced group:

Normal distribution tests for the advanced group						
	Kolmogorov-Smirnov			Shapiro-Wilk		
Task	Statistics	df	Significance	Statistics	df	Significance
Logging_AO	,323	6	,050	,776	6	,035
Logging_OO	,215	6	,200	,924	6	,537
Parameter Null_AO	,142	6	,200	,984	6	,969
Parameter Null_OO	,212	6	,200	,909	6	,433
Synchronization_AO	,271	6	,194	,798	6	,056
Synchronization_OO	,231	6	,200	,871	6	,231
Player Check_AO	,285	6	,138	,825	6	,097
Player Check_OO	,383	6	,006	,718	6	,009
Notify Observers_AO	,257	6	,200	,816	6	,081
Notify Observers_OO	,279	6	,160	,856	6	,174
Observers Null_AO	,303	6	,089	,755	6	,022
Observers Null_OO	,377	6	,008	,658	6	,002
Refresh Constraint_AO	,234	6	,200	,895	6	,345
Refresh Constraint_OO	,257	6	,200	,835	6	,119
Label Value Check_AO	,278	6	,161	,874	6	,243
Label Value Check_OO	,313	6	,068	,819	6	,086
Level Check_AO	,330	6	,040	,750	6	,020
Level Check_OO	,366	6	,012	,731	6	,013

Table 5-23 – Results for normal distribution tests for the advanced group

Now, only the Player Check and the Observers Null task pairs fall out of the picture, as for at least one of their two values one of the H0 hypotheses does not hold and has to be rejected. They therefore do not qualify for a t-test and cannot be considered normally distributed. The other seven pairs can now be tested using a dependent pair-samples t-test[1] in the next step.

- H0:   The expected time required to fulfill the task using the object-oriented language is the same as the time required for the fulfillment of the task using the aspect-oriented language.
- H1:   The expected times of object-oriented and aspect-oriented languages differ.

---

[1] http://en.wikipedia.org/wiki/Student%27s_t-test

In this case, the expected time manifests in the means for the tasks.

					T-Test			
		std.	std. error	95% confidence interval				Sig. (2-
	mean	derivation	mean	lower	upper	T	df	tailed)
Logging	-2034,50000	934,12542	381,35511	-3014,80451	-1054,19549	-5,335	5	,003
Param Null	-384,50000	45,62346	18,62570	-432,37888	-336,62112	-20,644	5	,000
Synchronization	-135,83333	144,74311	59,09113	-287,73191	16,06524	-2,299	5	,070
Notify Observers	314,66667	350,42584	143,06075	-53,08269	682,41603	2,200	5	,079
Refresh Constraint	255,50000	94,42616	38,54932	156,40582	354,59418	6,628	5	,001
Label Value Check	473,00000	197,98182	80,82574	265,23082	680,76918	5,852	5	,002
Level Check	119,00000	169,37887	69,14863	-58,75222	296,75222	1,721	5	,146

Table 5-24 – Results for the paired T-tests on the tasks of the advanced group that are supposedly normally distributed

For the Logging, Parameter Null, Refresh Constraint and Label Value Check tasks the hypotheses H0 does not hold and has to be rejected, meaning that there is a significant difference among the times for the aspect-oriented and object-oriented technique among the advanced group. For the Logging and Parameter Null tasks the confidence intervals lie between about -3000 to -1000 and -432 to -336, indicating an overall good result for aspect-oriented programming. H0 does hold for the Synchronization, Notify Observers and Level Check tasks, so it seems that there are no significant differences for these times in the advanced participants group. Their absolute values seem to not differ as much from each other as the values from the tasks where H0 does not hold do.

		N	ranks	rank sum	Z	asymptotic significance (2-tailed)
Logging	neg. ranks	0	,00	,00	-2,201	0,028
	pos. ranks	6	3,50	21,00		
Param Null	neg. ranks	0	,00	,00	-2,207	0,027
	pos. ranks	6	3,50	21,00		
Synchronization	neg. ranks	1	2,00	2,00	-1,782	0,075
	pos. ranks	5	3,80	19,00		
Player Check	neg. ranks	6	3,50	21,00	-2,201	0,028
	pos. ranks	0	,00	,00		
Notify Observers	neg. ranks	5	4,00	20,00	-1,992	0,046
	pos. ranks	1	1,00	1,00		
Observers Null	neg. ranks	5	4,00	20,00	-1,992	0,046
	pos. ranks	1	1,00	1,00		
Refresh Constraint	neg. ranks	6	3,50	21,00	-2,201	0,028
	pos. ranks	0	,00	,00		
Label Value Check	neg. ranks	6	3,50	21,00	-2,201	0,028
	pos. ranks	0	,00	,00		
Level Check	neg. ranks	5	3,40	17,00	-1,363	0,173
	pos. ranks	1	4,00	4,00		

Table 5-25 – Results for the Wilcoxon-test on all tasks for the advanced group

In addition to the t-test, the results for the Wilcoxon-test were calculated, the hypotheses being nearly the same:

- H0: The median of the times required to fulfill the task using the object-oriented language is the same as the median of the times required for the fulfilling the task using the aspect-oriented language.
- H1: The expected time medians of the object-oriented and aspect-oriented languages differ.

When looking at the results, one can see that for the Synchronization and the Level Check task, the H0 hypothesis holds, which is the same outcome as the t-test. But this time, H0 is rejected for the Notify Observers task, even if it is a close call. For all other tasks the hypothesis is rejected, too. The rank sums speak in favor of the object-oriented approach for all the smaller tasks, but is better for aspect-orientation among the larger tasks, which is where the advanced developers group had good overall results.

As a conclusion, only for the Logging, Parameter Null, Refresh Constraint and Label Value Check the results are significant in both tests.

Tests for the average group

The hypotheses for all tests in this group are similar to those of the advanced group, so they are not explicitly listed here anymore and the evaluation starts with the results from the tests for normal distribution.

Normal distribution tests for the average group						
	Kolmogorov-Smirnov			Shapiro-Wilk		
Task	Statistics	df	Significance	Statistics	df	Significance
Logging_AO	,198	9	,200	,947	9	,653
Logging_OO	,161	9	,200	,931	9	,492
Parameter Null_AO	,345	9	,003	,675	9	,001
Parameter Null_OO	,279	9	,041	,808	9	,025
Synchronization_AO	,175	9	,200	,944	9	,620
Synchronization_OO	,198	9	,200	,864	9	,107
Player Check_AO	,287	9	,031	,764	9	,008
Player Check_OO	,205	9	,200	,963	9	,828
Notify Observers_AO	,292	9	,026	,707	9	,002
Notify Observers_OO	,238	9	,150	,800	9	,020
Observers Null_AO	,191	9	,200	,931	9	,493
Observers Null_OO	,158	9	,200	,959	9	,788
Refresh Constraint_AO	,269	9	,059	,844	9	,064
Refresh Constraint_OO	,230	9	,186	,787	9	,015
Label Value Check_AO	,211	9	,200	,907	9	,296
Label Value Check_OO	,141	9	,200	,979	9	,960
Level Check_AO	,357	9	,002	,689	9	,001
Level Check_OO	,138	9	,200	,973	9	,916

Table 5-26 - Results for normal distribution tests for the average group

This time, the H0 hypothesis does not hold for the Parameter Null pair, the Player Check pair, the Notify Observers pair and the Level Check pair. These are probably not from a normally distributed population and therefore do not qualify for usage with the t-test. The t-test results are only calculated for the remaining tasks where H0 holds:

	T-Test							
				95% confidence interval				
	mean	std. derivation	std. error mean	lower	upper	T	df	Sig. (2-tailed)
Logging	-1722,22222	1754,08336	584,69445	-3070,53005	-373,91439	-2,946	8	,019
Synchronization	104,66667	366,28643	122,09548	-176,88601	386,21934	,857	8	,416
Observers Null	468,22222	402,85878	134,28626	158,55755	777,88689	3,487	8	,008
Refresh Constraint	361,77778	305,99828	101,99943	126,56668	596,98887	3,547	8	,008
Label Value Check	2459,11111	1329,00014	443,00005	1437,55117	3480,67105	5,551	8	,001

Table 5-27 - Results for the paired T-tests on the tasks of the average group that are supposedly normally distributed

H0 has to be rejected for the Logging, Observers Null, Refresh Constraint and Label Value Check tasks, meaning that these are supposedly the pairs of result sets that significantly differ from each other. When trying to explain why H0 holds for the Synchronization task, it appears that the differences between the development times for this task were not as big in this developer group. The confidence interval only speaks clearly in favor of the aspects for the Logging task.

		N	ranks	rank sum	Z	asymptotic significance (2-tailed)
Logging	neg. ranks	1	3,00	3,00	-2,31	0,021
	pos. ranks	8	5,25	42,00		
Param Null	neg. ranks	3	7,00	21,00	-0,178	0,859
	pos. ranks	6	4,00	24,00		
Synchronization	neg. ranks	6	5,17	31,00	-1,007	0,314
	pos. ranks	3	4,67	14,00		
Player Check	neg. ranks	9	5,00	45,00	-2,666	0,008
	pos. ranks	0	,00	,00		
Notify Observers	neg. ranks	9	5,00	45,00	-2,666	0,008
	pos. ranks	0	,00	,00		
Observers Null	neg. ranks	7	5,86	41,00	-2,192	0,028
	pos. ranks	2	2,00	4,00		
Refresh Constraint	neg. ranks	9	5,00	45,00	-2,666	0,008
	pos. ranks	0	,00	,00		
Label Value Check	neg. ranks	9	5,00	45,00	-2,666	0,008
	pos. ranks	0	,00	,00		
Level Check	neg. ranks	9	5,00	45,00	-2,666	0,008
	pos. ranks	0	,00	,00		

Table 5-28 - Results for the Wilcoxon-test on all tasks for the average group

For the Wilcoxon-test the H0 hypothesis holds only for the Parameter Null and the Synchronization task. As was already said, the differences especially for the larger tasks are not as big as in the advanced group. But the hypothesis holds for the Logging and all other tasks, which supports the result from the t-test. Only the Parameter Null and Synchronization task do not display significant differences in the resulting times.

All in all, this group exhibits significant results only for the Logging and the smaller tasks. It can be speculated that this group has not been created based on useful assumptions (solving two of three larger tasks with a positive result for aspect-orientation) and has not a strong enough correlation among the different participants' results.

Tests for the novice group

The novice group was the smallest group with only five participants, so the results of the tests do not have a high power.

Normal distribution tests for the novice group						
	Kolmogorov-Smirnov			Shapiro-Wilk		
Task	Statistics	df	Significance	Statistics	df	Significance
Logging_AO	,247	5	,200	,867	5	,254
Logging_OO	,383	5	,016	,713	5	,013
Parameter Null_AO	,306	5	,141	,810	5	,098
Parameter Null_OO	,154	5	,200	,982	5	,946
Synchronization_AO	,184	5	,200	,971	5	,882
Synchronization_OO	,242	5	,200	,937	5	,641
Player Check_AO	,208	5	,200	,908	5	,454
Player Check_OO	,229	5	,200	,920	5	,533
Notify Observers_AO	,315	5	,117	,835	5	,152
Notify Observers_OO	,317	5	,113	,811	5	,100
Observers Null_AO	,347	5	,049	,760	5	,037
Observers Null_OO	,260	5	,200	,869	5	,261
Refresh Constraint_AO	,213	5	,200	,913	5	,485
Refresh Constraint_OO	,311	5	,128	,850	5	,195
Label Value Check_AO	,233	5	,200	,890	5	,355
Label Value Check_OO	,213	5	,200	,940	5	,663
Level Check_AO	,216	5	,200	,930	5	,596
Level Check_OO	,408	5	,007	,656	5	,003

Table 5-29 - Results for normal distribution tests for the novice group

The hypothesis of normal distribution does not hold and has to be rejected for the Logging and Level Check pairs. These two will be excluded for the t-test. For all other tasks the hypothesis holds for both tests and they can now be included in the t-test.

For the t-test, the hypothesis has to be rejected for the Synchronization, Player Check and Label Value Check tasks, meaning their results are significantly different. For all other tasks the hypothesis holds and no significant difference can be detected.

| | T-Test | | | | | | | |
| | mean | std. derivation | std. error mean | 95% confidence interval | | T | df | Sig. (2-tailed) |
				lower	upper			
Parameter Null	-442,00000	461,88743	206,56234	-1015,50900	131,50900	-2,140	4	,099
Synchronization	744,60000	372,22748	166,46519	282,41853	1206,78147	4,473	4	,011
Player Check	328,00000	200,69629	89,75411	78,80264	577,19736	3,654	4	,022
Notify Observers	1265,00000	1265,77348	566,07111	-306,66536	2836,66536	2,235	4	,089
Observers Null	592,00000	805,41325	360,19175	-408,05263	1592,05263	1,644	4	,176
Refresh Constraint	121,80000	178,86643	79,99150	-100,29201	343,89201	1,523	4	,203
Label Value Check	1595,80000	1016,32903	454,51616	333,86083	2857,73917	3,511	4	,025

Table 5-30 - Results for the paired T-tests on the tasks of the novice group that are supposedly normally distributed

The novice group only consists of five result sets and in this case, for those tasks where the hypothesis has been rejected, some of their times do not differ much from each other, possibly explaining the results. Most confidence intervals are in a positive range, tending towards a favorable interpretation for the object-oriented technique.

		N	ranks	rank sum	Z	asymptotic significance (2-tailed)
Logging	neg. ranks	4	3,25	13,00	-1,483	0,138
	pos. ranks	1	2,00	2,00		
Param Null	neg. ranks	0	,00	,00	-2,023	0,043
	pos. ranks	5	3,00	15,00		
Synchronization	neg. ranks	5	3,00	15,00	-2,023	0,043
	pos. ranks	0	,00	,00		
Player Check	neg. ranks	5	3,00	15,00	-2,023	0,043
	pos. ranks	0	,00	,00		
Notify Observers	neg. ranks	5	3,00	15,00	-2,023	0,043
	pos. ranks	0	,00	,00		
Observers Null	neg. ranks	4	3,50	14,00	-1,753	0,080
	pos. ranks	1	1,00	1,00		
Refresh Constraint	neg. ranks	4	3,00	12,00	-1,214	0,225
	pos. ranks	1	3,00	3,00		
Label Value Check	neg. ranks	5	3,00	15,00	-2,023	0,043
	pos. ranks	0	,00	,00		
Level Check	neg. ranks	4	3,25	13,00	-1,483	0,138
	pos. ranks	1	2,00	2,00		

Table 5-31 - Results for the Wilcoxon-test on all tasks for the novices group

The H0 hypothesis for the Wilcoxon-test holds for the Logging, Observers Null, Refresh Constraint and Level Check tasks. For the Parameter Null, Synchronization, Player Check, Notify Observers and

Label Value Check tasks it has to be rejected. The Wilcoxon test outcome supports the t-test results for the Synchronization, Player Check, Observers Null, and Refresh Constraint tasks, but contradicts the results in regard to the Parameter Null and Notify Observers task (H0 gets rejected here). The only tasks that seem to have a significantly different set for both tests are Synchronization, Player Check and the Label Value Check.

To conclude this chapter, it seems that the grouping test outcome is rather confusing. There is no pattern in the significance of the results, as the number and type of tasks which have a significant difference seems to occur randomly or from a cause not yet understood or thought of. This might originate from the fact that the grouping assumptions are not correct (as already said) and the grouping is therefore faulty in respect to the overall results of the participants and their times. Especially the average and novice group have to be thought over, as their results seem to be random. Secondary, the grouping splits the data into even smaller groups where the test results are marginal at best and a lot more participants would have been needed for really significant results on the groupings. Only for the advanced developers group the results were significant for the first two larger tasks (Logging and Parameter Null), which is a good result because it strengthens the impression one gets from the absolute and ratio data. This means for the advanced group there is a significant difference in both approaches which largely results in a positive outcome for aspect-orientation. For the Synchronization task, the results are ambiguous and do not have a significant tendency into one direction. For all groups, only the Refresh Constraint and Label Value Check display a tendency similar to the first two larger tasks (even if it gets rejected on Wilcoxon for the novices group). All in all, grouping results are ambiguous for the average and novice group and are at least fairly enlightening for the advanced group.

6. Discussion

6.1.Thoughts on Validity

6.1.1. Internal Validity

For this experiment, one can identify many possible threats to internal validity, which might be due to its overall complexity and the complexity of collecting, processing and assessing data about the process of software development.

It begins with the data from the questionnaire, which seemed to have no general correlation with the results from the evaluation. The only explanation seems that some excellent or good developers where a little modest in their self-assessment and some average developers overestimated their own skills and experience. This is a general problem of questionnaires and subjective self-assessment. The results of the attempted groupings using the questionnaire data were not shown, but did not result in anything useful anyway.

The tutorial that was given to each participant could also have influenced the results. Great care was taken in trying to present the tutorial the same way each time, but as it was an interactive learning session, where participants could ask questions and make notes as well as try out on a tutorial workspace, the more interested and motivated participants might have profited more from the tutorial than others. They might have asked more questions and probably could link the new contents to existing knowledge better. The tutorial was also possibly much too short for some to get a feeling for the new technique.

To sum up, the participants skills seemed to differ a lot from each other, even if this did not show in the questionnaire results, which did not only manifest in the ambiguous experiment results but could also be perceived while supervising the experiment and the progress of some participants as wall as in the evaluation of the video footage.

Additionally, the overall progress of some participants was perhaps influenced by two other conditions: First, it could have happened that some participants misunderstood the task description and therefore had problems solving the task or used the wrong approach. They were told to read the task description and then ask if anything was not clear, but it could still have happened that some made mistakes because of a wrong sense for the task to do. Second, the participants were not grouped according to their answers to the skill questions in the questionnaire (which probably would not have helped much, because most assessed themselves very similar) but were rather randomly given first the aspect-oriented tasks or the object-oriented ones. It is possible that those who were given the object-oriented task first were later already familiar with the buildup of the application and had an impression of how the classes and methods looked, which might have helped in writing the necessary aspects. They might even have thought about how to write the aspect while doing the object-oriented part to save time later. This learning effect could have modified the experiments results. The learning effect could also have had an impact on the larger tasks, which were the first to work at and would have suffered the most from a possible initial time of adjustment.

Another effect might be that some participants had errors in their code and possibly had a hard time removing them to finally complete the task, even if their solutions to the task were already nearly or fully complete. The probability that such a problem could have significantly influenced the experiments outcome is low.

Looking at the smaller tasks, the different approaches taken by the participants pose a problem. Like straight copy and paste or find and replace, which altered the overall statistical results for the smaller tasks.

There is also the matter of how the real development time was measured and calculated. The timestamps were saved very precise by the development logging tool, but the evaluation had (because of technical limitations) to be limited to 30 second intervals for the larger tasks and five seconds for the smaller ones. This could be the source of overall small derivations from the exact results, but could not have had a significant impact, especially on the larger tasks. A little more of a problem is the calculation of the real development time from the timestamp where the developer first touched the code and the time all test cases were fulfilled completely. The ending point of test case fulfillment makes sense, but it can be discussed whether it was a good and appropriate idea to take the first code touch as a starting point, because it does not take the time for thinking about the task or participants accidently hitting a key into account. Some could possibly have touched the code before they even read the task description. Hence, the sense of this approach is at least debatable.

A last word on the values for the ratios and break-even points: It is discussable if they are meaningful values, because there probably is a correlation of the overall development skills of a participant and the results for both techniques, which means that in general, developers are proportional as fast using object-orientation as they are using object-orientation. This fact could have lead to high break-even values and ratios, because most developers had to match an extremely fast object-oriented time using a new technique, which could have been the source of the phenomenon that only those who were familiar with aspects managed to beat these times.

All these thoughts on inner validity are speculative and could only have had a very small impact on the results, as great care was taken to control all noise factors and most ambiguous results definitely appear because of the small participant count.

6.1.2. External Validity

The external validity of the experiments is threatened by the ambiguous and only moderately significant results. They will potentially only be transferable in respect to the larger tasks and the performance of the advanced developers who had some experience with aspects or were good at adjusting to the new technique. With a very high probability it can be stated that aspect-orientation does not make sense for redundant code tasks below a certain method count to be edited (if time is the only concern). This threshold value cannot be determined exactly, but it might lie around the value of 30 methods and also depends on the rate of change that needs to be done to the code and the aspect complexity.

There is no general transferability of the results for the average and novice developers who used aspect-orientation for the first time. It would be interesting to find out whether there is a specific point from which on developers can get productive using aspect-orientation.

6.2. General Discussion

Those who have examined the tasks carefully might have noticed that the object-oriented tasks do not really use the features which are commonly associated with object-orientation, like inheritance and polymorphism. The tasks required code to be written that was almost procedural. But the focus here lay on the redundancy and the development time, not the comparison of programming features. That way, the results are true for a comparison of both procedural and object-oriented code. Also, the tasks all consisted of rather constructed situations which would not appear in this form in real life projects (except possibly for the three larger tasks). But as was already mentioned, the focus laid on the redundancy, and writing redundant code lines or adding redundant code lines to a number of methods is a standard task in everyday programming. As was said in the motivation chapter, aspect-orientation had its source in these problems of crosscutting concerns which had an impact on many classes or components and would have to be inserted manually at the specific locations in class or component code. Taking this thought a little further, this is exactly what has been measured in this experiment.

The solely focus on the development time which was taken in the experiment can be criticized, because the development time is only one factor in software engineering and never should be the only focus when developing applications, as fast code production does not (at least not necessarily) result in quality code. All the other possible advantages (like better modularization of crosscutting concerns) and disadvantages (like a more complicated debugging) that aspect-orientation brings were completely blanked out for the sake of maximum control on the experiments variables. But this does not mean that there could be no synergy effects among these facets, as using an aspect to replace redundant code in a program could also insert modularization and better readability in the program structure. To go even further, one could state that when using aspect-orientation to replace redundant code in one's application, one gets better modularization, flexibility and readability for free (at least if some care is taken writing the aspect).

One danger of aspects is the temptation of putting everything that does not belong into a specific class or that can be solved faster using aspect-orientation into an aspect, possibly tangling the final program structure with join-points up to the point where no one knows the exact program flow anymore and debugging gets a burden and a nuisance. Even if it is perfectly fitting that developers change their strategy when knowing about the advantages of aspects, it could also lead to developers getting lazy writing the class methods and functions, because they know they can later easily insert code into all of them if needed to ("why should I make a null reference check on all reference parameters in my methods if I can later write an aspect to do that?"). It is also pretty easy to completely destroy the program flow and function with inserting one wrongly written aspect, and it can take a potentially long time to find such errors. This means debugging aspect-oriented applications should be researched thoroughly and an attempt has already been made (see the related work chapter). Another thing that has to be considered is the time the AspectJ compiler and the weaving add to the building of projects, which can be very cumbersome if many aspects are woven into the code. This impact could be felt noticeably even in this small experiment environment.

To stay realistic, no experiment can control and measure all these different aspects at once, and the advantage of time was that it is a quantitative value and can be measured easily and reliably (when leaving the thoughts about the definition of the real development time from above aside), making it possible to work with the data statistically. Most other quality criteria for software are not or at least not easily measurable in quantitative terms and often require subjective assessment of developers. Many people casually talk about modularization, flexibility, readability, reusability, maintainability etc. of their applications and do not even know how to exactly define or measure these software attributes[1]. Most of them are empty word shells (some even call them buzzwords) used in pretty presentations. They might stay that way until they can be at least partially quantified and measured to a degree that is intersubjectively unambiguous.

---

[1] A meta study on software measurement can be found in (Kleinschmager, 2008)

A lesson learned for the experiment setup is that it would be much wiser to try to even more restrict the environment and implementation of possible future experiments, as there have been too many possible noise variables influencing the experiments results (as can be seen from the discussion on validity above), even if most possibly only had a very minimal impact, if they had one at all.

Nevertheless, the greatest care was taken for the setup and implementation of the experiment as to not threaten the results. So, the experiment was a good first step towards understanding the impact of aspect-oriented programming, its uses and limitations. Interested scientists can use the data as well as the experiment setup and tools to replicate or further develop the experiment (or create completely new ones) and bring forward the empirical insights on the topic. The results presented in this work represent only a small portion of the mass of data that was really collected during the experiments implementation and the data is open to any other kind of evaluation that can make sense for further studies. For example, the data provided some interesting insights into the progress and performance of developers when writing object-oriented (or possibly procedural) code. Eventually, the goal should be to extend the understanding of aspect-oriented and object-oriented programming and their impact on writing code in as many aspects as possible, as there are still way too few experiments and results on software development available. The evolution of aspect-oriented programming itself is also still going on, and the integration of aspect-oriented techniques into industry or science software projects has only just begun.

7. Related Work

In the same year they published their paper on aspect-oriented programming, Kiczales and his colleagues presented a case study (Mendhekar, et al., 1997), where they showed that using aspect-oriented programming does not necessarily need to lead to degraded performance in programs and that the performance of object-oriented and aspect-oriented software can be equal when using the right optimization techniques. They used aspect-oriented programming to optimize an image processing system where the object-oriented approach had lead to the optimizations being sprinkled across the code.

Two years later, the experiments of (Walker, et al., 1999) were the first to be conducted using aspect-oriented programming and compared the performance of different developer groups on specific tasks, where one group used the AspectJ language and another used the object-oriented control language Java for comparison. They used an explorative and qualitative approach and their experiment was focused more on measuring ease of debugging and ease of change in programs and left the developers more freedom in the solving the tasks. The two studies concentrated on the developers' ability to find and fix faults in a program and on the ease of changing an existing system. The AspectJ language was very young at that time (version 0.1 was used, as stated in their paper) and has made a large step forward in evolution since then. One of their results was that using aspect-orientation provides better overall development performance when there is a clear separation of concerns between the functionality of the aspect and the rest of the program. They also concluded that *"aspect languages should enable the writing of aspect code that has a well-defined scope of effect on core functional code and that suitably encapsulates a concern"*[1].

In the same year, Martin Lippert and Cristina Videira Lopes conducted their study (Lippert, et al., 1999) on the effect aspect-oriented programming has on exception detection and handling using the AspectJ language. They used an existing Java Framework and reengineered its exception handling and detection using aspect-oriented programming. One of their conclusions was *"that AspectJ supports implementations that drastically reduce the portion of the code related to exception detection and handling"*[2]. They also discovered some weaknesses in the AspectJ version used (0.4) and made suggestions for potential improvement.

2004, (Colyer, et al., 2004) conducted a case study on the use of aspect-orientation in middleware approaches and large scale commercial projects and tried to use aspect-orientation to implement

---

[1] (Walker, et al., 1999), p.10
[2] (Lippert, et al., 1999), p.11

crosscutting concerns in a product line (among them the famous logging functionality). They proposed some improvements to the AspectJ compiler and the AJDT developer tools and concluded that with some improvements to performance and the available development tools, aspect-oriented programming can and will play an important part in handling software complexity in large-scale projects.

(Li, et al., 2006) did a case study on building commercial of the shelf (COTS) components using aspect-oriented programming. They investigated the process of building an easy to change COTS system using aspect-oriented programming. They said they could confirm the main benefit of aspect-orientation, that being the centralization of changes in the system and the removal of dependencies. Their conclusion was that aspect-orientation does not necessarily lead to fewer lines of code needing to be modified when reengineering applications, even if fewer classes have to be modified. A comparable study was done by (Papapetrou, et al., 2004), who assessed the development of a high-performance web system using and not using aspect-oriented programming. They found out that the two solutions did not differ in facets like performance, correctness or stability, but in the development time of the system and modularity of the code, which were both much better for the aspect-oriented system. Their results therefore speak in favor of aspect-orientation when considering development time, as was done in this work, even if the results in this work are more ambiguous.

Another related approach is the study on the maintainability of aspect-oriented software (Bartsch, et al., 2007), where a small group of developers had to carry out maintenance tasks on and aspect-oriented (AspectJ) and object-oriented (Java) system. Their results seem to suggest a slight advantage for the object-oriented system, as the developers were able to solve the tasks faster, but they did not seem to be significant. No difference between the understandability of both systems was discovered, although the participants were all new to aspect-oriented programming.

The study of (Greenwood, et al., 2007) focused on the design stability of an aspect-oriented system and (Coelho, et al., 2008) performed a study on language specific features, but both were unfortunately not available for reading, so no details can be given.

The main difference between most of those approaches and the approach taken in this experiment is that the focus lies only on the development time and no other desirable software attributes.

8. Conclusion

In this work, a controlled experiment was presented which compared the use of aspect-oriented constructs for the purpose of replacing redundant object-oriented code with the corresponding specification. In the experiment, the participants performed nine tasks on an object-oriented program using an object-oriented language as well as an aspect-oriented.

It was tried to refine, analyze and explore the data in many ways, but none of them showed a perfectly clear picture. Still, the data analysis revealed some interesting facts which will have to be explored and hardened in future experiments.

The experiment showed that for larger tasks (the real definition of large is rather unclear here, but can be suspected in the area of about 30 methods to be edited with similar to identical redundant code) the aspect-oriented approach turns out to be useful, while for rather simple tasks it potentially causes additional overhead (in terms of development time), which sometimes exceeds the time needed using the traditional approaches by more than 100% or values far greater. This was the case for most participants.

Altogether, it should be mentioned that empirical knowledge, especially in the area of aspect-orientation, hardly exists and controlled experiments are rather rare. Hence, the here presented experiment cannot be considered as a final answer to the question of how beneficial aspect-orientation is (when concentrating only the time facet). Instead, this should rather be considered as a first and necessary step in order to explore a large field. And apart from time savings, aspect-orientation introduces many additional benefits and drawbacks that will have to be examined in other experiments, like the dynamic features of aspect-orientation which were not part of this experiment's focus.

9. Appendix

9.1. The questionnaire

Fragebogen zum Programmierexperiment

Allgemeine Angaben

Vorname:

Nachname:

Studiengang:

Fachsemester:

Fragen zu Programmierkenntnissen

Wie würden Sie Ihre Programmierkenntnisse generell einschätzen?

Sehr gering ○ ○ ○ ○ ○ ○   Sehr erfahren

Wie viel Erfahrung haben Sie nach eigener Einschätzung in der Programmierung mit Java ?

Keine   ○ ○ ○ ○ ○ ○   Sehr viel

Wie viel Erfahrung haben Sie nach eigener Einschätzung in der Nutzung der Eclipse Entwicklungsumgebung?

Keine   ○ ○ ○ ○ ○ ○   Sehr viel

Wie bewerten Sie Ihre Kenntnisse in der Programmierung mit AspectJ?

Nie genutzt ○ ○ ○ ○ ○ ○   Sehr gut

Wieviel Zeilen AspectJ Quelltext haben Sie schon geschrieben? Grobe Schätzung:

○ <1.000   ○ <5.000   ○ <10.000   ○ <25.000   ○ <50.000   ○ >50.000

Haben Sie AspectJ bereits im Rahmen von Industrieprojekten eingesetzt?

○ Ja ○ Nein

Haben Sie AspectJ bereits im Rahmen von Forschungsprojekten eingesetzt?

○ Ja ○ Nein

Wenn Sie bereits Erfahrung damit gemacht haben, als wie nützlich erachten Sie AspectJ?

Nutzlos   ○ ○ ○ ○ ○ ○   Sehr nützlich

Figure 9-1 – Page 1 of the questionnaire

Mit welchen zusätzlichen Programmiertechniken außer der objektorientierten sind Sie schon in Berührung gekommen? Bitte angeben mit welcher Technologie die Erfahrung zusammenhangt. (z.B. logische Programmierung - Prolog)

Programmiertechnik	Technologie

☐ Element einfügen

Mit welchem sonstigen Programmiersprachen und den entsprechenden Entwicklungsumgebungen haben Sie bereits gearbeitet? (z.B. C= und Visual Studio 2008)

Programmiersprache	Entwicklungsumgebung

☐ Element einfügen

Fragen zu universitären Leistungen

Bitte geben Sie (falls vorhanden) die Noten in den folgenden Fachern an:

Programmierung

Nebenlaufiges Rechnen / Nebenlaufige Programmierung

Hier können sie sonstige Facher und dortige Noten angeben, die Sie geschrieben haben, und welche im Zusammenhang mit Ihren Programmierkenntnissen stehen:

Fach	Note

☐ Element einfügen

Figure 9-2 – Page 2 of the questionnaire

9.2. The aspect-oriented task descriptions

Aufgabenstellungen zum Programmierexperiment

Allgemeine Hinweise:

- Die Aufgaben bitte in der angegebenen Reihenfolge durcharbeiten und nicht versuchen, die Bearbeitung in anderer Reihenfolge durchzuführen.
- Bitte keine neue Aufgabe anfangen bevor die vorherige nicht abgeschlossen wurde.
- Die folgenden Aufgaben sind nur über einen Aspekt zu lösen
- Für die Überprüfung der Ergebnisse liegen für jede Aufgabe Testfälle vor, die ausgeführt werden können, um zu überprüfen ob die Anforderungen erfüllt sind. Die Bearbeitung der nächsten Aufgabe kann erst begonnen werden, wenn die Testfälle der vorherigen positiv getestet werden. Die Testfälle liegen im entsprechenden *test package.

- Die zu bearbeitenden packages sind: game, gui und filesystem. Die packages testing und *test sind nur für Bearbeitungszwecke gedacht, die dort enthaltenen Dateien sind in den Aspekten <u>nicht</u> zu berücksichtigen.
- Konstruktoren sind generell <u>nicht</u> zu bearbeiten.
- Die Aspekte liegen als Rahmenvorgabe bereits im package *test des Workspaces und müssen nur mit der entsprechenden Logik gefüllt werden.

Log Task:

Es sollen für jede Methode in der gegebenen Klassenbibliothek gewisse Informationen zu Debuggingzwecken mitgeloggt werden. D.h. für jede Klasse (Ausgenommen Interfaces und Enums) muss <u>jede</u> Methode (aber <u>keine</u> Konstruktoren) mit zusätzlicher Logging-Funktionalität versehen werden.

Für diese Aufgabe steht die Logger Klasse bereit, die die statische Methode log anbietet. Die log Methode hat die folgende Signatur:

```
log(String classname, String methodname,
 String returntype, Object [] paramarray, String [] paramtypes)
```

- String classname:
  o Der Name der Klasse (z.B. „Player"), welche die Methode enthält
- String methodname:
  o Der Methodenname der Methode in der der Log Aufruf stattfindet (z.B. „setPosition")
- String returntype:
  o Der Rückgabewert der Methode als String, z.B. „int"
- Object [] paramarray:
  o Die an die Methode übergebenen Argumente sind in einem Array zu speichern und zu übergeben. Werden an die Methode z.B. eine Integer und eine String Variable übergeben, so sind beide in das paramarray zu legen und zu übergeben. Hat die Methode keine Parameter, ist ein leeres Array zu übergeben. Die Reihenfolge, in der die Variablen an das Array zu übergeben, muss die gleiche sein wie die der Methodensignatur.
- String [] paramtypes:
  o Zusätzlich zu den Variablen, die im oben genannten Array gespeichert werden, ist ein String Array zu übergeben, welches die Typen der Instanzen der Parametervariablen als String speichert. Wichtig ist hierbei, dass die gleiche Reihenfolge eingehalten wird wie beim oberen Array.

Das folgende Beispiel soll die Nutzung der Log-Methode verdeutlichen. Es wird in der Methode tueEtwas(int x, int y) der Klasse Tester ein Eintrag eingefügt. Der Log-

Eintrag ist am Anfang der Methode vor allen anderen Codezeilen einzufügen, damit beim Logging keine Informationen verloren gehen:

```
public void tueEtwas(int x, int y) {
    Logger.log("Tester", "tueEtwas", "void",
        new Object[] { x, y }, new String [] { "int", "int" });

    //restlicher Methodencode
}
```

Die Log-Methode und ihre Parameter sind auch im Quellcode mit Dokumentation versehen, um die Bearbeitung zu unterstützen.

Die Aufgabe soll nur mit einem Aspekt gelöst werden, nicht durch Bearbeitung der Klassen selbst! Die Folien zu Join Point Daten und Reflection sind hier hilfreich.

Param Null Task:

Für alle Methoden in der Klassenbibliothek gilt es zu überprüfen, ob an die Methode übergebene Variablen von Referenztypen (dazu gehört auch String) nicht `null` sind. Der in den Methoden enthaltene Code darf nur ausgeführt werden, wenn alle übergebenen Referenzvariablen nicht `null` sind. Ist ein übergebener Parameter doch `null`, so soll eine neue `InvalidGameStateException` geworfen werden. Methoden die keine Parameter oder keine Referenztypen als Parameter enthalten sind bei dieser Aufgabe auszulassen. Beispiel:

```
public void tueEtwas(Object args) {
    if (args == null) throw new InvalidGameStateException();
    //restlicher Methodencode
}
```

Die Aufgabe soll nur mit einem Aspekt gelöst werden, nicht durch Bearbeitung der Klassen selbst!

Synchronize Task:

In den Klassen `GameObject`, `Player`, `Trap` und `GameLevel` sind zu Synchronisierungs-zwecken alle Methoden mit einem Synchronisierungsmechanismus zu versehen. Der Inhalt der gesamten Methode muss dabei in einen `synchronized(this) { }` Block verschoben werden. Beispiel:

```
public void tueEtwas(Object args) {
    synchronized(this) {
        //restlicher Methodencode
    }
}
```

Die Aufgabe soll nur mit einem Aspekt gelöst werden, nicht durch Bearbeitung der Klassen selbst!

Player Check Task:

In allen `update*(Player playerarg)` Methoden der Klasse `GameManager` ist als Konsistenzcheck zu überprüfen, dass der übergebene Player (playerarg) dem Player entspricht, auf den die `GameManager` Klasse mit der globalen Instanzvariablen `player` verweist. Ist dem nicht der Fall, so muss eine `InvalidGameStateException` geworfen werden.

```
public void updateMyPlayer(Player args) {
    if (args != player) throw new InvalidGameStateException();
    //restlicher Methodencode
}
```

Die Aufgabe soll nur mit einem Aspekt gelöst werden, nicht durch Bearbeitung der Klassen selbst!

Notify Obs Task:

In allen Methoden der Klassen `Player` und `GameObject`, die auf Instanzvariablen der Klassen schreiben (allerdings <u>kein</u> Konstruktor und <u>nicht</u> die addObserver Methode), ist nach jedem Setzen einer Instanzvariablen ein `notifyObservers()` abzusetzen. In allen anderen Methoden ist nichts zu ändern. Beispiel:

```
public void setzeWerte(int wert1, int wert2) {
    //sonstiger Methodencode
    x = wert1;
    notifyObservers();
    //sonstiger Methodencode
    y = wert2;
    notifyObservers();
}
```

Die Aufgabe soll nur mit einem Aspekt gelöst werden, nicht durch Bearbeitung der Klassen selbst!

Obs Null Check Task:

Vor dem Absetzen jedes **notifyObservers** in den bereits bearbeiteten Methoden der `Player` und `GameObject` Klassen (allerdings <u>kein</u> Konstruktor und <u>nicht</u> die addObserver Methode) ist zu prüfen, ob die Instanzvariable `observers` mit der Liste der `Observer` nicht gleich `null` ist. Ist sie gleich `null`, so ist eine `InvalidGameStateException` zu werfen. Beispiel:

```
public void setzeWert(int wert) {
    //restlicher Methodencode, der den Wert setzt und sonstige
    //Logik ausführt
    if (observers == null) throw new InvalidGameStateException();
    notifyObservers();
}
```

Die Aufgabe soll nur mit einem Aspekt gelöst werden, nicht durch Bearbeitung der Klassen selbst!

Refreshconstraint Task:

In allen `refresh*` Methoden der `LabyrinthFrame` Klasse ist zu prüfen, ob die übergebenen Werte nicht < -1 sind. Ist dies doch der Fall, so soll eine `InvalidGameStateException` geworfen werden. Wichtiger Hinweis: Da die getArgs() Methode ein Object Array zurückgibt, können die Werte der darin gekapselten primitiven Typen nur über folgendes Verfahren geholt werden (im Beispiel mit Integer):
`((Integer)thisJoinPoint.getArgs()[i]).intValue()`

Die Aufgabe soll nur mit einem Aspekt gelöst werden, nicht durch Bearbeitung der Klassen selbst!

Label Value Check Task:

In den `refresh*` Methoden (welche einen Labeltext setzen) der `LabyrinthFrame` Klasse ist zu überprüfen, ob das letzte Zeichen des Strings des gesetzten Labels nach dem Setzen das Leerzeichen " " oder eine Integer Zahl ist. Ist dies doch der Fall, so soll eine `InvalidGameStateException` geworfen werden. Dafür existiert die Methode `isValidLabelString(String text)`, an den der Text der Labels übergeben werden kann. Beispiel:

```
public void refreshValue(int value) {
    //restlicher Methodencode
    if (!isValidLabelString(valuelabel.getText()))
        throw new InvalidGameStateException();
}
```

Die Aufgabe soll nur mit einem Aspekt gelöst werden, nicht durch Bearbeitung der Klassen selbst!

Level Check Task:

Es wird in der GameManager Klasse an diversen Stellen die Instanzvariable `currentlevel` neu gesetzt. Bei allen diesen Operationen (ausser in der setLevel Methode) soll vorher überprüft werden, ob der neu zu setzende Level von seinen Dimensionen größer ist als der alte Level. Ist dem nicht so, so soll eine `InvalidGameStateException` geworfen werden. Als Hilfe existiert die `GameManager` Methode `checkLevelConstraints(GameLevel newlevel, GameLevel oldlevel)`, die ein `true` für einen erfolgreichen Check oder `false` bei Fehlschlag zurückgibt.

Beispiel:

```
public void levelSetzen(GameLevel newlevel) {
    //restlicher Methodencode
    if (!checkLevelConstraints(newlevel, currentlevel))
        throw new InvalidGameStateException();
    currentlevel = newlevel;
}
```

Die Aufgabe soll nur mit einem Aspekt gelöst werden, nicht durch Bearbeitung der Klassen selbst! Es ist zu beachten dass die currentlevel Variable manchmal null sein kann.

9.3.The object-oriented task descriptions

Aufgabenstellungen zum Programmierexperiment

Allgemeine Hinweise:

- Die Aufgaben bitte in der angegebenen Reihenfolge durcharbeiten und nicht versuchen, die Bearbeitung in anderer Reihenfolge durchzuführen.
- Bitte keine neue Aufgabe anfangen bevor die vorherige nicht abgeschlossen wurde.
- Für die Überprüfung der Ergebnisse liegen für jede Aufgabe Testfälle vor, die ausgeführt werden können, um zu überprüfen ob die Anforderungen erfüllt sind. Die Bearbeitung der nächsten Aufgabe kann erst begonnen werden, wenn die Testfälle der vorherigen positiv getestet werden. Die Testfälle liegen im entsprechenden *test package.
- Die zu bearbeitenden packages sind: game, gui und filesystem. Die packages testing und *test sind nur für Testzwecke gedacht, die dort enthaltenen Dateien sind in den Aufgaben nicht zu bearbeiten.
- Konstruktoren sind generell nicht zu bearbeiten.
- Die Aufgaben bitte nur objektorientiert lösen.

Log Task:

Es sollen für jede Methode in der gegebenen Klassenbibliothek gewisse Informationen zu Debuggingzwecken mitgeloggt werden. D.h. für jede Klasse (Ausgenommen Interfaces und Enums) muss jede Methode (aber keine Konstruktoren) mit zusätzlicher Logging-Funktionalität versehen werden. Für diese Aufgabe steht die Logger Klasse bereit, die die statische Methode log anbietet. Die log Methode hat die folgende Signatur:

```
log(String classname, String methodname,
  String returntype, Object [] paramarray, String [] paramtypes)
```

- String classname:
  - Der Name der Klasse (z.B. „Player"), welche die Methode enthält
- String methodname:

- o Der Methodenname der Methode in der der Log Aufruf stattfindet (z.B. „setPosition")
- `String returntype`:
  - o Der Rückgabewert der Methode als String, z.b. „int"
- `Object [] paramarray`:
  - o Die an die Methode übergebenen Argumente sind in einem Array zu speichern und zu übergeben. Werden an die Methode z.B. eine Integer und eine String Variable übergeben, so sind beide in das paramarray zu legen und zu übergeben. Hat die Methode keine Parameter, ist ein leeres Array zu übergeben. Die Reihenfolge, in der die Variablen an das Array zu übergeben, muss die gleiche sein wie die der Methodensignatur.
- `String [] paramtypes`:
  - o Zusätzlich zu den Variablen, die im oben genannten Array gespeichert werden, ist ein String Array zu übergeben, welches die Typen der Instanzen der Parametervariablen als String speichert. Wichtig ist hierbei, dass die gleiche Reihenfolge eingehalten wird wie beim oberen Array.

Das folgende Beispiel soll die Nutzung der Log-Methode verdeutlichen. Es wird in der Methode `tueEtwas(int x, int y)` der Klasse `Tester` ein Eintrag eingefügt. Der Log-Eintrag ist am Anfang der Methode vor allen anderen Codezeilen einzufügen, damit beim Logging keine Informationen verloren gehen:

```
public void tueEtwas(int x, int y) {
    Logger.log("Tester", "tueEtwas", "void",
        new Object[] { x, y }, new String [] { "int", "int" });

    //restlicher Methodencode
}
```

Die Log-Methode und ihre Parameter sind auch im Quellcode mit Dokumentation versehen, um die Bearbeitung zu unterstützen.

Param Null Task:

Für alle Methoden in der Klassenbibliothek gilt es zu überprüfen, ob an die Methode übergebene Variablen von Referenztypen (dazu gehört auch String) nicht `null` sind. Der in den Methoden enthaltene Code darf nur ausgeführt werden, wenn alle übergebenen Referenzvariablen nicht `null` sind. Ist ein übergebener Parameter doch `null`, so soll eine neue `InvalidGameStateException` geworfen werden. Methoden die keine Parameter oder keine Referenztypen als Parameter enthalten sind bei dieser Aufgabe auszulassen. Beispiel:

```
public void tueEtwas(Object args) {
    if (args == null) throw new InvalidGameStateException();
    //restlicher Methodencode
}
```

Synchronize Task:

In den Klassen GameObject, Player, Trap und GameLevel sind zu Synchronisierungs-
zwecken alle Methoden mit einem Synchronisierungsmechanismus zu versehen. Der Inhalt
der gesamten Methode muss dabei in einen synchronized(this) { } Block verschoben
werden. Beispiel:

```
public void tueEtwas(Object args) {
    synchronized(this) {
        //restlicher Methodencode
    }
}
```

Player Check Task:

In allen update*(Player playerarg) Methoden der Klasse GameManager ist als
Konsistenzcheck zu überprüfen, dass der übergebene Player (playerarg) dem Player
entspricht, auf den die GameManager Klasse mit der globalen Instanzvariablen player
verweist. Ist dem nicht der Fall, so muss eine InvalidGameStateException geworfen
werden.

```
public void updateMyPlayer(Player args) {
    if (args != player) throw new InvalidGameStateException();
    //restlicher Methodencode
}
```

Notify Obs Task:

In allen Methoden der Klassen Player und GameObject, die auf Instanzvariablen der
Klassen schreiben (kein Konstruktor und nicht die addObserver Methode), ist nach jedem
Setzen einer Instanzvariablen ein notifyObservers() abzusetzen. In allen anderen
Methoden ist nichts zu ändern. Beispiel:

```
public void setzeWerte(int wert1, int wert2) {
    //sonstiger Methodencode
    x = wert1;
    notifyObservers();
    //sonstiger Methodencode
    y = wert2;
    notifyObservers();
}
```

Obs Null Check Task:

Vor dem Absetzen jedes **notifyObservers** in den bereits bearbeiteten Methoden der
Player und GameObject Klassen (kein Konstruktor und nicht die addObserver Methode)
ist zu prüfen, ob die Instanzvariable observers mit der Liste der Observer nicht gleich

null ist. Ist sie gleich null, so ist eine InvalidGameStateException zu werfen. Beispiel:

```
public void setzeWert(int wert) {
    //restlicher Methodencode, der den Wert setzt und sonstige
    //Logik ausführt
    if (observers == null) throw new InvalidGameStateException();
    notifyObservers();
}
```

Refreshconstraint Task:

In allen refresh* Methoden der LabyrinthFrame Klasse ist zu prüfen, ob die übergebenen Werte nicht < -1 sind. Ist dies doch der Fall, so soll eine InvalidGameStateException geworfen werden. Beispiel:

```
public void refreshValue(int value) {
    if (value < -1) throw new InvalidGameStateException();

    //restlicher Methodencode
}
```

Label Value Check Task:

In den refresh* Methoden (welche einen Labeltext setzen) der LabyrinthFrame Klasse ist zu überprüfen, ob das letzte Zeichen des Strings des gesetzten Labels nach dem Setzen das Leerzeichen " " oder eine Integer Zahl ist. Ist dies doch der Fall, so soll eine InvalidGameStateException geworfen werden. Dafür existiert die Methode isValidLabelString(String text), an den der Text der Labels übergeben werden kann. Beispiel:

```
public void refreshValue(int value) {
    //restlicher Methodencode
    if (!isValidLabelString(valuelabel.getText()))
      throw new InvalidGameStateException();
}
```

Level Check Task:

Es wird in der GameManager Klasse an diversen Stellen die Instanzvariable currentlevel neu gesetzt. Bei allen diesen Operationen (ausser in der setLevel Methode) soll vorher überprüft werden, ob der neu zu setzende Level von seinen Dimensionen größer ist als der alte Level. Ist dem nicht so, so soll eine InvalidGameStateException geworfen werden. Als Hilfe existiert die Methode checkLevelConstraints(GameLevel newlevel, GameLevel oldlevel), die ein true für einen erfolgreichen Check oder false bei Fehlschlag zurückgibt. Beispiel:

```
public void levelSetzen(GameLevel newlevel) {
    //restlicher Methodencode
    if (!checkLevelConstraints(newlevel, currentlevel))
        throw new InvalidGameStateException();
    currentlevel = newlevel;
}
```

10. References

Bartsch, Marc and Harrison, Rachel. 2007. An exploratory study of the effect of aspect-oriented programming on maintainability. *Software Quality, 2007.* 2007.

Basili, Victor and Zelkowitz, Marvin. 2007. Empirical Studies - to build a science of computer science. *Communications of the ACM, Vol. 50, No.11, p. 33 - 37.* 2007.

Basili, Victor. 2007. The role of controlled Experiments in Software Engineering Research. *Empirical Software Engineering Issues, LNCS 4336, pp. 33 – 37.* 2007.

Bortz, Jürgen and Döring, Nicola. 2002. *Forschungsmethoden und Evaluation, 3. überarb. Auflage.* s.l. : Springer-Verlag, 2002.

Christensen, Larry B. 1977. *Experimental Methodology.* s.l. : Allyn and Bacon, 1977.

Coelho, Roberta, et al. 2008. Assessing the Impact of Aspects on Exception Flows: An Exploratory Study. *ECOOP 2008: 207-234.* 2008.

Colyer, Adrian and Clement, Andrew. 2004. Large-scale AOSD for Middleware. *AOSD 04.* 2004.

Greenwood, Phil, et al. 2007. On the Impact of Aspectual Decompositions on Design Stability: An Empirical Study. *Proceedings of ECOOP 2007, pp. 176-200.* 2007.

Hanenberg, Stefan. 2005. *Design Dimensions of Aspect-Oriented Systems.* 2005.

Highley, T.J., Lack, Michael and Myers, Perry. 1999. Aspect-Oriented Programming: A critical analysis of a new programming paradigm. *Technical Report: CS-99-29.* 1999.

Jones, C. 1994. Gaps in the object-oriented paradigm. *Computer,Volume 27, Issue 6, p.90-91.* 1994.

Josupeit-Walter, Manuel. 2008. *Empirische Forschung an Objektorientierung.* Essen : University Duisburg-Essen, Chair of Data Management Systens and Knowledge Representation, 2008.

—. 2009. *Entwicklung eines Eclipse Plugins zur Aufzeichnung der Aktivitäten eines Entwicklers.* Essen : University Duisburg-Essen, Chair of Data Management Systens and Knowledge Representation, 2009.

Kiczales, Gregor, et al. 2001. An Overview of AspectJ. *Proceedings of the 15th European Conference on Object-Oriented Programming, Vol. 2072, pp. 327 - 353.* 2001.

Kiczales, Gregor, et al. 1997. Aspect-Oriented Programming. *Proceedings European Conference on Object-Oriented Programming, Vol. 1241, pp. 220-242.* 1997.

Kleinschmager, Sebastian. 2008. *Software Metrics for Empirical Studies of Programming Language Features.* Essen : University Duisburg-Essen, Chair of Data Management Systens and Knowledge Representation, 2008.

Li, Jingyue, Kvale, Axel Anders and Conradi, Reidar. 2006. A Case Study on Improving Changeability of COTS-Based Systems using Aspect-Oriented Programming. *JOURNAL OF INFORMATION SCIENCE AND ENGINEERING 22, 375-390.* 2006.

Lippert, Martin and Videira Lopes, Cristina. 1999. *A Study on Exception Detection and Handling.* 1999.

Mendhekar, Anurag, Kiczales, Gregor and Lamping, John. 1997. *RG: A Case-Study for Aspect-Oriented Programming.* 1997.

Papapetrou, Odysseas and Papadopoulos, George A. 2004. Aspect Oriented Programming for a component-based real life application: A case study. *SAC 2004.* 2004.

Prechelt, Lutz. 2001. *Kontrollierte Experimente in der Softwaretechnik.* s.l. : Springer-Verlag, 2001.

Rogge, Klaus-Eckart. 1995. *Methodenatlas für Sozialwissenschaftler.* s.l. : Springer-Verlag, 1995.

Steidley, C.W. 1994. The object oriented paradigm: issues and practices. *Northcon/94 Conference Record, p. 148 - 152.* 1994.

Tichy, Walter. 1997. Should computer scientists experiment more? *Computer, Volume 31 , Issue 5, p. 32-40.* 1997.

Walker, Robert J., Baniassad, Elisa L.A. and Murphy, Gail C. 1999. An Initial Assessment of Aspect-oriented Programming. *Proceedings of the 21st International Conference on Software Engineering.* 1999.